ADVANCE PRAISE FOR *In My Own Moccasins*

"An incredible debut that documents how trauma and addiction can be turned into healing and love. I am in awe of Helen Knott and her courage. I am a fan for life. Wow."
—RICHARD VAN CAMP, author of *The Lesser Blessed*

"Heartfelt, heartbreaking, triumphant, and raw, *In My Own Moccasins* is a must-read for anyone who's ever felt lost in their life." —JOWITA BYDLOWSKA, author of *Guy: A Novel* and *Drunk Mom*

"An intelligent, courageous, emotionally searing account."
—GLOBE AND MAIL

"A searingly honest self-portrait." —TORONTO STAR

"A powerful exploration of a family, colonialism, and the potential for redemption and healing." —WINNIPEG FREE PRESS

"Proclaims healing a revolutionary act . . . . Knott's complex portrait evokes empathy for those struggling with addiction and opens a window into a story that makes space to tell abuse survivors they are not alone, it is not their fault, and she will remember them." —BOOKLIST

In My Own Moccasins

A Memoir of Resilience

Helen Knott

Printed and bound in Canada at Marquis. The text of this book is printed on 100% post-consumer recycled paper with earth-friendly vegetable-based inks.

COVER AND TEXT DESIGN: Duncan Noel Campbell
COPY EDITOR: Alison Jacques, PROOFREADER: Donna Grant
COVER ART: Portrait of Helen Knott (detail) by Tenille Campbell
FEATHER GLYPH: by Karla Design from the Noun Project.

Library and Archives Canada Cataloguing in Publication

Title: In my own moccasins : a memoir of resilience / Helen Knott.

Names: Knott, Helen, 1987- author. | Robinson, Eden, writer of foreword.

Series: Regina collection ; 11.

Description: Series statement: The Regina collection ; 11 | Foreword by Eden Robinson.

Identifiers: Canadiana (print) 20190105445 | Canadiana (ebook) 20190105461 | ISBN 9780889776449 (hardcover) | ISBN 9780889776456 (PDF) | ISBN 9780889776463 (HTML)

Subjects: LCSH: Knott, Helen, 1987- | CSH: Native women—British Columbia—Biography. | LCSH: Recovering addicts—British Columbia—Biography. | LCSH: Victims of crimes—British Columbia—Biography. | CSH: Native women—Canada—Social conditions | CSH: Native peoples—Canada—Social conditions. | LCGFT: Autobiographies.

Classification: LCC E78.B9 K56 2019 | DDC 971.1004/970092—dc23

University of Regina Press

Saskatchewan, Canada, s4s 0A2
TEL: (306) 585-4758 FAX: (306) 585-4699
WEB: www.uofrpress.ca

10 9 8 7 6 5 4 3 2

We acknowledge the support of the Canada Council for the Arts for our publishing program. We acknowledge the financial support of the Government of Canada. / Nous reconnaissons l'appui financier du gouvernement du Canada. This publication was made possible with support from Creative Saskatchewan's Book Publishing Production Grant Program.

Offering and Dedication

MY TRUTH IS ALL THAT I HAVE. TRUTH IS MY OFFERING.

This is for the women who cannot remember and for those who choose not to.

To the women who still believe that it is all their fault. To the women who have been abused and violated and then forced to wear the heavy garment of shame afterward. To the women whose spirits are struggling to hold light. To the women who have had the gift of life taken from them. To the women whose lines between consensual and forced are blurred by society's perceptions of them. To the women who suffer silently and slip away, leaving their stories untold. To the women who feel as though they deserved it, who were told that they asked for it by their manner, their speech, or their dress. To the women who have been forced to forget because of others who refuse to remember. To the women who have forgotten that they have the right to say no. To the women whose bodies hold tales no living creature should ever be told.

I give you this acknowledgement for your memories. I give you soft-spoken prayers for your healing and courage for your spirits.

I give this in hopes that you remember that you are worth a thousand horses.

I remember.

This is my offering.

—HELEN KNOTT, OCTOBER 18, 2018

Contents

Foreword
By Eden Robinson

IN JANUARY 2016, I WAS FOLLOWING THE PROTESTS of BC Hydro's Site C Dam in the Northeast corner of British Columbia's Peace River Valley. Through mutual acquaintances, I noticed Helen Knott's posts appearing in my Facebook feed. Helen, a young Indigenous woman, was about to set up the Rocky Mountain Fort protest against Site C along with farmers who were also going to be impacted by the impending construction and flooding.

As my father's reserve had been slated to be the terminus of the Enbridge Northern Gateway pipeline, and we'd been fighting it for what felt like forever, I was deeply invested in the Rocky Mountain Fort protest camp, and especially with Helen Knott. Her writing was immediate, heartfelt, and powerful. She contextualized her connection with her land so poetically that, when the protest ended and the camp was logged, I was gut-wrenched. I have followed Helen Knott since, and she is a powerhouse.

What an honour to be asked to write this foreword. In a time when new Indigenous authors are blazing through the literary heavens, this memoir shows her not only to be a gifted writer but also a compelling leader, an emerging matriarch unafraid of engaging with the political machinery of Canada and the world.

In My Own Moccasins never flinches. The story goes dark, and then darker. We live in an era where Indigenous women routinely go missing, our youth are killed and disposed of like trash, and the road to justice doesn't seem to run through the rez. Knott's journey is familiar, filled with the fallout of residential school, racial injustice, alcoholism, drugs, and despair. But she skillfully draws us along and opens up her life, her family, and her communities to show us a way forward. It's the best kind of memoir: clear-eyed, generous, and glorious. As she grows into her strength she writes:

Healing yourself is a revolutionary act.
Healing yourself is the ultimate act of resistance.

The memoir you're holding is her testimony. Her story can be harsh, but it's full of compassion and, ultimately, triumphantly surging with life and urgency. Bear witness to the emergence of one of the most powerful voices of her generation.

Introduction

SOMEONE, SOMEWHERE, ONCE TOLD ME THAT A SONG will travel the world until someone is ready to receive it. Since then, I have imagined stories and poetry roaming the earth. Right now, invisible words are being carried by gusts of wind trying to find someone to bring them into this world. Metaphors and similes are wandering the streets looking for a home.

I did not catch this story riding in on a breeze or stumble into it in the grocery aisle while looking to complete my shopping list. I have lived this story. I had to pull this story out of body, out of bone, out of a place so deep that it does not have a name.

I have spent a lot of time in a state of healing and retrieval to be able to write these words and give them to the world.

I have also spent a lot of time in a state of reflection, examining my own intentions behind giving these words to the world.

There are moments when I realize that one day this book will be in someone's hands and I can feel the butterflies rise from my belly to my throat. I am a girl again on an old wooden roller coaster awaiting the first plummet toward the ground. My heartbeat quickens. I wonder if I should have gotten on the ride. My palms sweat. I question if I was meant to write the book.

Then I remember.

Yetchay kay nusgee.

I remember things from long ago.

I remember all the women who held space for me while I worked to erase the records of violence that my body held. I know there are women out there with similar stories, with records on their body that have not been erased yet. I have sat with women who have been silenced, whose intergenerational lines of violence stretch themselves in an attempt to reach another generation. I have sat with women who have had to have vaginal reconstruction surgeries and women who have been ostracized because of their quick tongues and demands for justice.

I remember these women.

I wrote this for you.

I remember the sweaty hands and contorting body in crave of substance. I know that so many people are actively suffering from addiction. I know that other mothers are suffering from addiction. I have had a myriad of conversations with

individuals surrounding sobriety and healing. I have prayed
with strangers. I have hugged mothers who were trying to
become sober. I remember believing that I would never achieve
sobriety, and I write these words from this side of freedom.

I remember those who struggle with addiction.

I wrote this for you.

I remember what it was like to believe I was a dispens-
able Indigenous woman. I have sat with women who have
talked about scrubbing their skin trying to achieve white.
I have sat with women who have had to untangle the mess
that a lifetime of stereotypes and racism leaves behind. I
have held space for the sisters who had to weep and wail
away the colonial harm. I have held space for the sisters
whom we have lost to violence. I know that acts of violence
against Indigenous women and girls are being perpetuated
every single day.

I remember you, sisters.

I wrote this for you.

I have written this book from the intersection of these
three places of remembering. They are inseparable strands
braided together. Without each of them you would not have
the full story. I summoned these words and the healing that
comes with them to lighten the loads of shame, addiction,
and struggle.

I pray these words of remembering can somehow be
medicine for you.

I was told that this book will be a good tool to educate
people who do not understand the impact of violence, racism,

and colonialism in Indigenous women's lives. I was told that there will be people who gain insight from this book.

I did not write this for you.

I did not write this book so that people can learn how to humanize Indigenous women and gain context for the violence that seems to fill our lives. As an Indigenous woman, I once begged to be seen as a human. I promised myself I would never again beg for what is mine. I understand that your learning will be a by-product of these words, and that is a good thing. We must understand each other in order to change the world. I invite you into this space with an open heart and with the requirement that you burn your pity and bury your judgements.

As Indigenous women, we sometimes must unapologetically write for ourselves.

I wrote this for us.

Part One
The Dreamless Void

one

YOU CAN FEEL A MOTHER'S LAMENT IN HER VOICE. The tone of her words penetrates the skin and hits bone, it hits something deeper than bone, it hits spirit. The chest feels as if someone is pushing on it with brute force and that breath, that one breath, is a struggle to get in and get out. Remorse shapes the sounds leaving her mouth and they become a rough-edged grief-filled symphony, a mixture of wailing and words that cannot be unheard.

You wince.

You attempt to display no signs of your internal reactions to the shame that gets caught in her throat, but every hesitation in her story proves that silence can be a tangible beast as it forcibly pulls your head to a lowered position. You feel every struggled sentence as she speaks, or maybe you have to be a mother to feel it? Or maybe you have to be a mother who once neglected her own to feel it.

They almost lost me that time.

I almost lost myself.

I SHIVERED AS my sweat seeped through my clothing. I damned the light that intruded into the darkness of the room. The pillowcase that hung in the window frame was pinned sideways and the afternoon light came in across the room slanted. The same way my world felt.

Dust particles danced in the broken light. Laughter erupted from somewhere downstairs. The smell of stale cigarette smoke enveloped me. I clenched my eyes tightly, shifted, and moaned.

My detoxing body had me contracting into a tight ball one minute and expanding like a starfish the next. The floor was covered in clothes, some mine, some his. The mattress was on the floor, my heaped-up body on the mattress. My body pulled into itself. I wondered what it would be like to go through withdrawals somewhere pretty, somewhere clean. Somewhere where the outside didn't match my insides.

I was dying a slow self-inflicted death.

If I could get my hands on another bottle and a couple of lines of coke, I'd feel enough—or rather, not feel enough— to get out of the bed and catch a bus somewhere. I would go south to Revelstoke, where an old friend lived, or to the east where I knew some people.

Saskatoon. Winnipeg. Toronto. Somewhere.

I spent the days before trying to locate men who had known me when I was human. When I was sober. Men who had fallen for me when I was feminine and tender-hearted. Would they even recognize the woman I had become? I thought I could compel them to take care of me by appealing to their better nature or their long-standing urges to sleep with me. I would slip into arms that I knew could never hold me at my best. At the rate I was going I knew I couldn't possibly take care of myself. I was terrified.

I was eight hours from home, in Edmonton, a city more than thirty times the population of my small hometown, Fort St. John. I could easily slip into line with the nameless, the faceless, and the voiceless. That's why I went there. To erase myself. To crash into the other non-existents and melt into their ever-changing formation. People disappeared every day. Native women like me disappeared every day. Becoming an invisible Indigenous woman was a goal of manifest destiny that I was no longer willing to fight against. I had to vanish from the landscape of life and let myself become a missing poster, a candle lit at a Sisters in Spirit vigil, a single exhale of relief from white men on Parliament steps. I had no more fight left in me and I had convinced myself that everyone would be better off without me.

My mother, my dad, my son.

All of them would be better off with my absence rather than be scarred by my self-destruction. I would soon shape-shift into a black-hearted monster. I had seen this monster before. It looked like hidden mickeys of vodka in bookcases, perpetual bleeding noses, and bedside beers to keep the shaking hands and nightmares away.

I contracted. Expanded. Contracted.

I twisted the stained sheet around my body. I became a bed-bound aerial dancer performing without grace and with only my conscience for an audience. I pulled on it tight as if the tension of the sheet snaked around one leg and up around my neck could hold my body in place. It couldn't.

Contracting. Expanding. Contracting.

"Helen," Alex said, with a soft knock on the door. "You need to eat," he whispered, as he sat down beside me and placed a plate of chicken and berries by my head.

I only wanted a beer but I was too ashamed to ask. I didn't think Alex would have understood. I ate a handful of berries but my throat outright denied the chicken no matter how small of a bite I took. It lodged itself in my throat and I reached for the glass of water he had brought me earlier. My body trembled and when Alex noticed it, he looked away.

"You need sleep," he said, softly.

I felt my body contract and tensed my muscles to hold myself in position.

"Hold me?" I asked.

I was scared of losing my grip on reality. Scared to be alone. Terrified of the nightmares that were sure to follow.

Alex lay down beside me and wrapped his long pale arms around me.

Arms white like snow, my asu (grandmother) would say. White like *yuss*, she would say it in our language. I vibrated, and he held me tighter. His body became a straitjacket attempting to restrain my body's need to convulse. I felt as if my spirit was trying to break out of my skin. Maybe it was.

Minutes rolled by. An hour passed.

"Helen?" he whispered.

"Mmmm," I moaned in reply. Even full syllables and words were not without effort.

"Did you sleep at all?"

"No."

"Helen?"

"Mmmm."

"My shirt is soaked from your sweat."

After another hour of restraining me, and comforting me, with still no luck at sleeping, he left me to fight my own battle.

Contracting. Expanding. Contracting.

two

FIVE DAYS BEFORE I WAS STARFISHING IN ALEX'S BED, I was sitting at home, which also happened to be my parents' home. The house where I spent most of my teenage years. I had moved back in to their home after I had gotten accepted into a national Indigenous women's leadership program. It was supposed to be a new beginning.

But stories have a way of coming unearthed, no matter where you call home.

At that time, I was managing to keep the shifting ground beneath me still for long enough to catch my breath. My asu had been living with me for about a year by then, so when my son and I moved to my parents', she moved in too. After my papa had passed, Asu stayed alone in her large cream-coloured house an hour and a half outside of town at the Halfway River Reserve. The house sat on top of a hill on a dead-end dirt road and was the epicentre for our family functions. Their home was the heart from which we flowed and to which we found our way back. We never quite recovered from the loss of it as a family. It had a woodstove that kept it warm in −40°C winters and Papa forever had cords of wood stacked beside the house with endless rows continuing in the shed. Papa was a man of preparation. There were bird feeders scattered about the property that were filled even though Asu swore every single year that she was done feeding the birds. An old whisky jack would come along in the winter, cawing and such, and Asu just couldn't bear the thought of him going hungry. Poor magpies, poor whisky jacks, poor birds—but those chipmunks and squirrels had it rough. Asu always had a skinny log leaned up against a tree behind the house with copper wire wrapped and looped around it.

"What is all that for?" I asked her once, pointing at the brass-coloured circles of wire.

"It's to snare those damned squirrels. They're no good, they just chew up car wires," Asu replied scornfully as she waved her hand in dismissal of the now-obvious tiny looped snares.

Their house was one of the only homes on reserve that was fully fenced. Asu and Papa built that fence themselves over the course of a season. Papa would make them a lunch to go, a thermos of coffee and a sandwich with mashed potatoes and tomatoes (a union of food I never understood) or Spam with some butter. They would load into one of the trucks Papa had revived from somebody's backyard automobile cemetery and off they would go in search of thin trees that they would later peel and stain by hand for their fence.

They were tough old people.

When they knew we were coming for a visit, they prepared for our arrival. When we started driving up the dirt-road hill to their house and broke the first bend I could see a wisp of smoke rising up and I knew that the warmth of a home fire was waiting.

Reaching the top of the hill I would see Papa first. He was always wearing one of his striped long-sleeved shirts with suspenders and moving things around in the yard. When he saw us approaching, he yelled out to Asu, "Mom, they're here!"

Asu was usually out in the yard too, poking the fire with her long wooden pole. They would stop what they were doing and watch us pull up. A moment of stillness. A welcoming.

The firepit was at the mouth of a long narrow shelter structure they put together from wood, sheet metal, and thick plastic. Papa would take out old car seats from busted-up ancient automobiles and place them in the shelter with some old blankets to cover them. We would sit out there by the fire on our GMC seats and tell stories until all the stories were emptied on out of us and the lingering silences told us it was time to go to bed. I remember watching the fire's shadows dance on Papa's pale face as he stared at the flames trying to think of another story. He always looked so handsome, especially when he would emerge from the bathroom with his white hair slicked back, donning a plain white tee and black suspenders with the smell of Old Spice wafting from him.

When Papa was dying of cancer and finally got placed in the hospital for good, his face held that blue colour just beneath the skin. It was the kind of blue you catch when you are stuck outside in one of these northern winters for too long but that wasn't comparable by any means to his bright blue eyes. Those eyes held fast and bright through the entire sickness.

When he couldn't shave his own face anymore, I brought a razor and some shaving cream to the hospital and wheeled him to the bathroom. I spread the shaving cream out carefully over his stubbly jawline while Papa's eyes inspected my every move in the mirror. I grabbed the razor and heeded his warning not to use hot water on it because it would dull it "right quick boy." I pressed the razor to the outer corner of his jaw and dragged the blade a couple of inches toward his chin. I did this a few more times, cautious and conscious of the blade. Papa watched me politely but when he realized I was not going to pick up the pace and put any pressure to get that close shave he liked he huffed, "Push harder, you're not going to break me, goddammit."

We laughed and his blue eyes lit up.

We did not acknowledge that he was already broken.

I pushed harder and continued making maps across his face much like the backroads we used to criss-cross on our adventures when I was a little girl. Several of us kids would be jammed in a three-seater pickup, ducking when the police were spotted. We would stop somewhere and go trailing off into the bush. Papa would roll a cigarette and Asu would decipher animal tracks with us as we looked for berries or scouted for empty beer cans to be cashed in. Other times we'd perform bear watch when we went to the dump to rummage. One honk = a bear was spotted. Two honks = the bear was getting brave. Dump rummaging was one of my favourite things to do with Papa and Asu because you could find some really cool things as long as you didn't mind the smell of rotting stuff mixing with the earth. There were books, toys, Faith Hill cassette tapes. People threw away things that still served a purpose.

Papa was a tough smart-mouthed man who doubled as Asu's chauffeur and cook. Asu never drove a day in her life. Well, once—except she almost ran over Papa and never got behind the wheel again. Not long after he passed away I drove up to Asu's one autumn day and told her she was going to come live with me in town. She agreed. A year later, when I decided to make the move to my mom's, we had a hell of a time. Both Asu and I had to downsize our lives to fit into a small room. We were figuring out what items we could move into storage and what was necessary to take and Asu sat in her room overwhelmed by the years of items accumulated.

She, a devout Catholic, had various styles of crucifixes, Virgin Mary statues, and even the odd bottle of holy water floating about just in case someone was in need of a blessing or of a warding off of some spirits. One time, my youngest auntie and cousin accidentally drank her holy water. Asu always had it in inconspicuous bottles. A bottle of Buckley's turned into a sacred container. The only telling sign it was blessed water was usually small black writing somewhere on the bottle. *Holy water.* They drank that bottle dry before they saw the marking. All Asu had to say was that maybe they both had to stop swearing now on account of their mouths being blessed.

One of her crucifixes was big enough for a dwarf-sized Jesus to be on it. She had snagged it at a flea market years before, and it took up a good space of her bare white wall. Asu never bothered to close her blinds, either, so Giant Jesus could be seen hanging on her wall from down the block. With windows unobstructed and a lamp flicked on every single night, lit-up Jesus provided spiritual blessings and protection for all the neighbours.

"Helen," she said, sounding like a small girl, looking up at her wall at the huge cross.

"Yes?" I answered.

"Can I take Jesus?"

"Asu, you can take Jesus wherever you want!"

I laughed, she laughed, and Jesus probably smiled.

We packed up and moved ourselves a couple of blocks down.

My son and I shared a room in my parents' swelling brown house. His toys and my clothes were all jumbled together in the closet, spilling out onto the floor just a little on good days. A lot on most days. Asu had the room across the peeling-linoleum hallway and my parents' room was beside us. My youngest brother, who is the same age as my son, shared my parents' room. My oldest brother still occupied a room downstairs.

At least the house had a furnace then.

My son was born a few years before in mid-winter and was brought home into the swelling house. There was no furnace when he was an infant.

Winter is six months of the year in the North and the house was a bitter cold place to be. The floors would bite your feet and the rooms' chilly air would nibble at your cheeks. The oven door would be flipped down and glowing like the mouth of a hungry beast. That is, until the oven's element burned out too. Then, we would boil big pots of water on the two working burners for the warmth of evaporation. We knew all the tricks of in-house heat production. We spent a lot of our time trapped in our small rooms with a plug-in heater going. I joke about having thick skin after being raised in the North, but it was probably the winters in that house that did it.

A year after moving back with Asu, I was still there. I was fucking up six ways until Sunday and then skipped Sunday and added six more sins.

I sat listlessly on the couch as my son and youngest brother went for an overnight visit at one of my aunties'.

That's when the addict in me started to whale on the walls of my flesh and began rattling my bones.

I could feel my anxiety begin to pulse throughout my veins. It was Friday night and I had just spent the week at my job as the Aboriginal Education coordinator at the local college. I thought about the conversations that I'd had with two older students. Both of them had recently been through a treatment centre and I made a point to ask them about their red road journey and to encourage them. I would still be sick on Monday from a three-day-straight coke and alcohol binge and saying shit like "Sobriety is never easy, but you know what you need to do when you need to do it," or "Pray for the guidance you need and Creator will hear you." It was a ridiculous and incongruent ordeal but I still believed in sobriety, even after my relapse. I just didn't believe that it was possible for me anymore.

I was messing up—and I had no capacity to feel, let alone to have faith.

The weekend before, I had disappeared on Friday night, like many weekends before that. I'd come back sometime Sunday morning without sleep and without feelings. I'd passed out and woken up to Mom screaming at me and hitting my body.

"What the fuck is wrong with you? Do you know how many times your son comes into this room to check if you fucking made it home? Do you even care?!" she yelled.

I didn't know how to care anymore.

I cared even less since the incident.

The fuckin' incident. The blood. The voices that followed the blood. The tears that I didn't cry.

The death I carried inside of me since then.

It was something I still hadn't talked about.

But it was all I thought about at night and I couldn't lay in bed with those thoughts next to me.

The memories haunted me so much that I ran away to Edmonton—leaving my son behind.

Thinking I could appease them with my complete self-destruction.

I sat on the couch and flicked through the channels, watching my mom enter and exit the living room as she gathered her things. I left it on a black-and-white movie and stared at the dreamy face of a young Cary Grant. I had always wished I could live back in that era. But to live in that era and love it, I would have to be a middle-class white woman.

You couldn't be a poor Indian girl and experience anything these movies depicted.

I don't know if it is the dramatic romance that I loved about black-and-white classic movies but I would sometimes watch them when I was drinking alone. And I did this too often. A hopeless alcoholic addict and a hopeless romantic. Doubly fucked.

At least I wasn't drinking alone and watching horror and thriller movies. I'd be a hopeless alcoholic addict and a hopeless future cult leader and conspiracy theorist.

Drink the Kool-Aid. It's not poisoned, just spiked with a gallon of rum, and the communion is dusted with cocaine.

So I watched Cary Grant rattle off one of his well-articulated long script lines and I did not swoon. My internal feelers were definitely broken.

"Come to the casino with me," my mom said as she sprayed a citrusy-smelling perfume in front of her and walked through the mist. Her brown hair was teased, coiffed, and ready for a night of gambling.

"No," I shook my head.

"Why not? It'll get you out of the house."

"I'll drink."

"Oh Helen," she chided me. "You can do it without drinking. It's as simple as not having one."

"Okay, I'll go," I said, as I rose off the couch with every intention of having a drink when I got there.

My mom is an ex-alcoholic. You would think that she would know it was never that simple.

We arrived, and I spotted my friend Jennifer with her bright dyed-red hair, dressed in a white long-sleeved shirt, unbuttoned low. I hadn't seen her since St. Patrick's night when we'd gotten greened up and I'd introduced her to my drug-den gang. She had left before morning while I had stayed perched on the couch for two more days.

That was the difference between her and me. She knew when to go home. She remembered she was a mother.

The moment we arrived at the casino, my mom drifted off into the maze of binging and blipping slot machines as I walked toward Jennifer.

"Hey girl, what's up?" I said, pulling a stool to the table she was perched at.

"Just got off work," she said, raising her glass. "Waiting for my mom to come pick me up in an hour."

"Where you working?"

"The restaurant next door, total joke if you ask me but low shirts equal more tips. Didn't do half bad today," she said with a wink and we both laughed at the truth of it.

"Game of pool then?"

"Let's do it," she smiled.

We walked over to the pool tables and I was already eyeballing the waitresses, so they would come and take my drink order. I couldn't walk up to the place where the drinks were sold because it jutted out in the middle of the small casino and my mom would definitely see me. My drinking would not be spoiled—I couldn't have that, nor the agony of having only one rye and Coke.

As the Alcoholics Anonymous saying goes, one is too many and one hundred is never enough. I was aiming for one hundred. The pool tables were tucked away and private. I could drink there with ease.

Jennifer set up the pool balls and I pretended I was actually interested in playing pool.

Finally, the waitress walked over.

"Can I get you ladies anything to drink?"

"Rye and Coke please," I answered. "Actually, you better make that a double."

"I'll have another vodka with cranberry juice," Jennifer said as she cracked the cue and the balls split up across the table and two disappeared into the pockets.

"Oh snap, someone has her game face on," I said.

"That's right, bitches, I'm going to own this table!" she laughed.

Just then "I'm Real" by Ja Rule and JLo came on the speakers. Ja Rule's raspy voice yelled out something about his name and "the game" while JLo's smooth voice answered back. Jennifer's body swayed to the beat before her mouth opened.

"Girl, you remember dancing at the Galaxy to this track?!" she squealed.

The Galaxy was a teenage dance club that we used to go to. It had a short life in Prince George, where we both had lived when we were young. I heard it closed down after repeated fights and bricks being thrown through the window, but I did get to dance my heart out in it a few times before it shut down.

"Yup, that place beat dancing at that city youth centre place with the pat downs and sock checking for drugs," I replied. "That place was rough as fuck."

We weren't close friends at all, but we had history. Jennifer had just moved to Fort St. John but she was the first girl I met when I'd moved to Prince George years ago. I was living in that city because some sideways shit went down and I needed to disappear from Fort St. John. My life has been full of disappearing acts, and violence has always inspired them. I moved in with an auntie from my dad's side. I was thirteen.

MY ADOLESCENCE WAS riddled with turmoil and shaky soil.

I was in Grade 9. By this time, my addictions had become so pronounced they could no longer be called a habit. Addiction was my lifestyle and it manifested in hideous ways.

One night, after partying, I woke up in a hospital bed. I didn't know how I had gotten there. I blacked out. Again. The police officer asked for my name and I didn't want my mom showing up there so I said I was Abigail Johnson. They asked me how to get a hold of my mom. I told them I didn't know.

I didn't know why there were so many police officers around me. Or why I was in a hospital gown. I didn't know what was happening.

Abigail Johnson's mom showed up.

Abigail Johnson was a real person. A girl I went to school with. Drunk me should have thought that one out.

I can still picture Mrs. Johnson and her worried face at my bedside. Her wild unruly 4:00 a.m. hair, with a look of confusion and then a face of relief when she realized I was not her daughter. The police took the confused mother back on the other side of the curtains.

I saw my opportunity and tried to jump out of the bed while the police were distracted with her. I was still really drunk and had to grab onto things to make it down the hall.

I stumbled into the waiting area and I saw three boys sitting in some of the chairs. I walked closer and realized I recognized them.

"What are you guys doing here?" I said, completely oblivious that I stood there in a hospital gown.

"Helen," said Jack.

Jack was a boy from school. All three of them were Native boys that I knew from school. Jack looked concerned, his brow furrowed.

"I need to leave here, help me leave," I said, looking behind me. The policeman would be there soon.

"Helen," Jack said softly, "we found you. You were out by the railroad tracks, in the ditch. We thought you were dead, Helen."

"What? No," my head spun harder and I grabbed onto a chair. "No, that makes no sense."

Blackout.

I WAS IN the hospital bed again when I came to, and this time my mom was beside me. She was crying. I clenched my eyes shut. I didn't want to wake up. I didn't want to know what had happened. When she stopped crying I opened my eyes.

"My girl," my mom said, as she reached for my hand and squeezed it.

"Mom, can we go? I want to get out of here, take me out of here," I pleaded. I was scared.

"Just a second," she said as she got up and walked out into the hallway.

I could hear muffled voices outside.

"Just make sure you contact us this afternoon. We have questions for her," a man's voice said.

"Yes," replied my mom.

"I brought you clothes, my girl," she said as she pulled a bag onto the bed.

My body was sore and I moved slowly into my clothes while my mom helped dress me. I kept my eyes on the floor as we walked out. I didn't want to see people looking at me.

"Helen, what happened last night?" my mom said once we got into the car.

"I don't know," I said as I stared out the window.

"You have got to remember something, Helen," my mom's voice begged me.

"No, Mom," I said, my voice cracking. "I don't."

"They found you lying out in that ditch. If those boys didn't find you they said you would have died." My mom paused and took a deep breath. "You could have died, Helen. They said they think you were raped."

I heard her voice catching. She was crying. I wanted to disappear into the car, into the cement below, slip into the earth. I wanted to stop existing, to not hear the rest of the story.

"You were naked. Naked except for a sweater that was draped over you."

I said nothing. Tears rolled down my cheeks.

"Take me home," I whispered.

My feelings left my body. My spirit sat outside of me like an unacknowledged apparition. I didn't know whose life I was living, whose body I inhabited. This wasn't my story, my life, my reality. I felt like I could float away at any moment, but a vague awareness kept me nailed to the ground. It's a weird thing to disconnect from your body and your experiences and yet be present almost as a bystander. I was scared that if I tried to lean into my feelings I would fall off the emotional edge and I didn't know what I would do to myself.

I learned later in life that this is called dissociation.

I sat silently in the vehicle. The silence was harder to withstand than my mom's probing questions.

I had a hot shower when I got home, then a hot bath. I lay in the water motionless and silent. My tears rolled into the bathtub. I didn't want to come out. I hated myself for letting this happen to me.

I did this, I thought as I blinked back my tears.

Save the fucking tears for someone who deserves them.

I heard a soft knock at the door. I didn't answer. Another knock.

"What?" I murmured.

"We need to go back to the hospital, my girl. You need to come and get ready."

"For what?"

"They need to do some tests."

I dunked my head underwater. If only I could keep my head under long enough, I wouldn't have to come out. Another knock. I raised my head and swallowed air, then rose slowly from the water. My thighs were sore, my body ached. My mom had laid out clothes for me and I dressed myself.

"What kind of tests?" I asked when we got into the vehicle again.

"Some swabs and stuff. Just to, you know, check it out, and make sure you're okay."

"Some swabs? Where?"

"Down there. I don't know what else they're going to do but the police need it. You have to do it, my girl."

I stared out the window. Tears burned my cheeks, my chest roared as if a wildfire had been lit in its cage. I didn't know if I could survive being in my own body.

Stop crying, bitch, I scolded myself. Fuckin' stop it.

They put me in a small room. There was a lady officer there and she was cold, distant, and formal. The metal table gleamed. I could hear the chattering of the doctor and the officer and my mom. The door shut.

"You need to change into the gown," my mom said, holding it out to me. Her eyes held a fragile sadness and she held the gown out weakly. She helped me undress and tied the back of the gown for me. I lay down and she put a small knit blanket on me.

"Mom," I said, "I don't want to do this." This time my voice pleaded with her. "Mom, please."

My mom lowered her head and started to cry as well. Then she stopped crying and put on that brave face moms put on for their children and she grabbed my hand. "I know, my girl," she strained to get the words out. "But you need to, and Mommy will be right here. I'm right here."

The cop and the doctor came in. I turned my head toward the wall. They did what they needed to do. I heard the words "rape kit" and "vaginal-wall bruising." They confirmed among themselves that there was evidence of sexual violence. I flinched when they pulled pubic hairs out. I lay there silently. I gritted my teeth, clenched my jaw, and tried to blink my tears back.

"Did she have a shower?" the police officer asked, ignoring my presence.

"Yes," my mom answered.

"She really shouldn't have done that. We needed her to stay as she was. I don't even know if we will get anything from these swabs now," the officer reprimanded my mom, her voice distant.

"We didn't know, and I wasn't going to make her stay like that all day waiting for you to get this done," my mom said sternly.

Silence.

I STAYED AT home after that, but a few days later I wanted to go and get homework from school because I didn't want to fall behind. My mom drove me to the old brown-stone junior high, pulled into the dirt parking lot, and asked if I wanted her to go in with me.

"I can do it," I said.

I was halfway to the cafeteria when I realized that everyone knew what had happened to me. Small towns leave no room for secrets.

People stopped beside the aging orange lockers to stare at me as I walked past. Their whispers zipped through the air and broke down whatever loose barrier I had placed around me before coming in. My skin stung with shame.

A kid I had known since the sixth grade came running up to me with an amused look on his face. "Helen! Is it true?"

"What?" I asked.

"Did you get raped?!"

I lost my breath and the world started to twirl.

I pushed past him and into the cafeteria. A hush fell over the room and every eye turned in my direction. I started to hyperventilate and I wanted to disappear into the floor, disappear beneath the floor into the concrete, slip further down and into the earth. I became dizzy and made my way into the bathroom, pushing into people and pushing past them. I collapsed in a bathroom stall and began to cry.

I don't remember how long I sat there. I stayed in the stall until one of my friends came and found me and escorted me out. My mom was pacing outside.

We got into the vehicle and I broke down crying.

"I need to move, Mama," I howled. "Take me elsewhere, I can't live . . . I can't live here."

My body was shaking, and tears and snot flowed down my face.

My emotions forced themselves on me all at once and I wasn't capable of taking the inward assault.

I began hitting the dashboard and the windows as if hitting something would take me out of my body and stop whatever I was feeling. I thrashed about in the car seat. It felt like my spirit was trying to jump out of my body. I screamed. Mom's eyes were wide with terror.

"I can't fucking do it, I can't," I sputtered as my body crumpled into a ball and shook.

That is how I came to live in Prince George when I was a teenager.

This is how I had come to meet Jennifer.

It was not the beginning of sexual trespasses on my body and it was not the ending of rape in my life.

I HAD SIX drinks to Jennifer's four drinks before my mom left the slot machine long enough to find out what I was up to. I was a grown-ass woman who needed babysitting. She instantly started screaming at me and calling me names in front of anyone who was within earshot, which just happened to be all of the casino patrons. I shut down and numbed myself. Her words became meaningless blobs vacating her mouth.

I knew I was a fuck-up.

"Can't even stay sober for your own fucking son!" she yelled.

Before the comments registered, I walked away.

I needed obliteration.

So, I shifted into autopilot, got into a cab, and went to a seedy stripper bar downtown. The Condill, one of Fort St. John's buildings, was the end-of-the-line kind of bar where you could drink by yourself and not feel out of place. LMFAO's "Party Rock Anthem" was playing when I walked in, and the music was the only thing lending life to the overall ambience of hopelessness. This was not a place for Party Rocking. This was a place for at-the-table drug deals, fist fights, and sexually hungry oil and gas workers. The room smelled of urine and shame. The floor was stained, the stools wobbled, and the men were questionable.

I drank hard.

My phone buzzed and I read a text message from my auntie who was watching my son.

Your son wants you to come home now. Go home.

I'm a fucking loser, I thought as I put my phone back in my jacket pocket. A fucking grade A loser. I accepted it as fact and set out to forget it.

Jimmy, a guy I knew from way back, came and sat beside me. We hadn't seen each other in years and I wasn't surprised to see him here of all places.

"Want a drink?" he asked, with his small squinty eyes smiling at me.

"Always fuckin' do," I replied.

He was there with his girlfriend, who looked like she was there with three other men across the bar. We sat and bullshitted for a bit when he bought me a second drink and ordered himself a pop.

"What the fuck, Jimmy?" I said, pointing to his pop.

"Nah, I gotta stay sober to watch over my girl tonight. If you need a ride later, call me."

He gave me his number before he chased after his girl-friend, who had walked outside with another man.

"Hey." A guy approached me. "Don't I know you?"

It always starts that way with these kinds of men in places like this. You never know the character but it's easier for them than saying, "Hey, I'm a creep and I want to know you."

"Can I buy you a drink?" he asked.

"Let's just do a shot together," I replied.

"What kind?"

"Tequila—is there any other kind?"

"Tou-fuckin'-ché."

He bought the shots and let a growl out after downing his, like the tequila threatened his manhood. Apparently there is nothing more redeeming of one's masculinity than a primitive growl.

Then, a moment of truth.

My son's face flashed in the back of my mind. I felt a twinge in my stomach but I decided to drown it. I would never be the mother he deserves.

"One more," I said to the bartender.

"Hardcore, huh?" Don't-I-know-you guy said, smiling at me.

I shrugged my shoulders and took the shot.

I called Jimmy for a ride at closing but he didn't answer. Don't-I-know-you guy hovered nearby with predator-like skill and told me to come to his place. I wasn't ready to go home yet, so I went home with him. When we got to his place he poured me a drink and before the drink was done we started kissing. I knew he would want to have sex and I started to panic.

I had not had sex since my most recent rape. So now, even when I was drunk, I remembered to be worried. My phone buzzed. It was Jimmy.

"Where are you?"

"I'm at this guy's place . . ." I answered.

"Give me the address," he said. "I'm coming to get you."

I was relieved. I was grateful for Jimmy. I didn't want to lock lips anymore with Don't-I-know-you guy. I downed my drink and then stood outside in the cold, waiting for Jimmy. I stared at the soft, smooth cover of freshly fallen snow and the way that it caught the street light. The cold sparkle that would kill you if you decided to give yourself to it. I wanted to be swallowed by the stillness of it all.

My great-uncle was swallowed by it.

I remember looking for him with my mom on cold winter nights like this one.

We would drive up and down alleyways in our old pale blue Pontiac Bonneville as if we were playing a perpetual game of hide-and-seek. When we found him down some back alley he would always sing us a song at the top of his lungs and make me laugh.

"Livin' doll! How you doin'?!" he'd ask me in his thunderous voice. "You know why I call you livin' doll? Because when you were just a baby that's what you look like. A livin' doll, yep. My niece, the livin' doll," he'd say and I would giggle some more.

Mom would dig into her purse and give him some money, and then he would disappear down a quiet, blackened alleyway. I remember staring at his figure growing smaller from the back window until I couldn't see him anymore. He used to be a guide for hunters in the mountains, a damned good one, so I've been told. They called him Johnny Biscuits on account of all the biscuits he would eat up in the mountains.

"Oh Johnny Biscuits is stayin' out here for longer," the camp cook would say. "I better whip up double the biscuits now. Boy, that man can eat!"

I remember seeing a picture of him when he was young. He was holding up the head of a bighorn sheep he had shot, a smile on his beautiful brown face that boasted the sharp Bigfoot family nose. The streets and the liquor, though, they swallowed him and the mountains he left unconquered inside of him whole. I wanted to disappear like that. The moment broke when Jimmy pulled up and I walked over to his beat-up brown chariot and jumped in.

"Where to?" he asked.

"Cocaine," I said.

"Cocaine it is," echoed Jimmy.

We drove off into the night on a mission.

A HANDFUL OF dashboard lines, some cheap whisky, and three hours later we were sitting with another buddy from way back named Michael in his basement suite. Michael was still wiping the sleep out of his eyes when he handed me a Budweiser. The sun was up at that point and I could hear the birds chirping outside one of the windows. I cringed. The sound of life continuing on made me want to smash something. Not the beer, though. That would be an alcoholic sacrilege.

I drank the beer quickly and deliberately. It gave me the courage for what I knew I needed to do. I needed to leave town. I wouldn't keep fucking up. This was my fuck-up finale.

I went to the fridge and grabbed myself another bottle of beer. I had checked my bank account before we arrived. I had just over one thousand dollars and then another five hundred on my credit card. I had managed to keep two good jobs so far, but carrying on like this, it was bound to end sometime and the time was now.

"I'm going to Edmonton," I declared, as I popped off the top of the beer on the counter edge.

"For what?" Michael asked, his head cocked sideways.

Michael had had a crush on me since we were thirteen years old. I used to do silly things to make him blush, because he blushed so easily. He was a good guy but I had always seen him as a friend.

"I need to leave town," I said as casually as I could.

We all knew people who had to "leave town," so not a lot of explanation was needed but I wouldn't have given one even if they had asked.

"We could both go," offered Jimmy.

"I have to go there in a few days to pick up some parts," Michael said. "If you can wait, I'll drive you."

"Fuck that, I need to leave now."

Michael and Jimmy started talking out details while I cut up a couple of lines of coke.

I knew Michael had been trying hard to stay clean. I felt a stab of guilt as I leaned my head over the table. The guilt was gone as soon as the line was. Within a few hours we were on our way with a case of beer in the back seat and some old-time rock blaring on the stereo of a beat-up car.

We drank. We sang songs and joked around, rustling up decade-old stories and taking them for a spin. I reached my hand out the window and pushed the rear-view mirror inwards.

"What the hell are you doing?" Jimmy asked.

"I can't be looking back anymore," I said.

"You're a fucking trip, you know that?" he said, laughing and shaking his head.

"Where's your girlfriend anyways?" I asked.

"She's getting the last of her shit out of her system, you know? She's been hooked on a lot of different drugs, you fucking name it. It's been fucked up."

I snorted.

"What?"

"Well, Jimmy," I said, waving my hand around the vehicle, "we're kind of fucked up ourselves."

"Guys," Michael said from the back seat.

"Yeah?"

"You're kinda killing my buzz back here."

We all started laughing. I reached for the volume and turned up the boys of CCR singing about the Midnight Special shining a light on some shit or other. Michael lit a smoke. Jimmy bobbed his head. I motioned for Michael to pass me another beer.

"Don't you have fuckin' music that my mom didn't party to?" I quipped.

"Shut yer goddamn mouth. This is classic," Jimmy said as he turned it louder.

three

WHEN WE GOT TO EDMONTON, THE BOYS TOOK ME to the mall. I had left with nothing, and although the last place I wanted to be wasted at was a mall, I had no choice. I only had the clothes I was wearing and I wasn't ready to fully let my appearance metamorphose into the classic unkempt, un-showered alcoholic addict. If that was to come, it would be later down the line.

I was scared, though, because I knew I would eventually be at a street level of addiction.

I wasn't one of those fancy functioning alcoholics whom I heard stories from at Alcoholics Anonymous. The ones who could keep a job for thirty years and still drink themselves into a stupor every other night. I actually mildly envied that ability, because for me, when the beast came a-knockin' it would take everything. The fear of what would become my life gnawed at the back of my mind but I refused to answer to it.

"Well, fuck," Jimmy croaked. "We'll be waiting in the food court. I ain't pickin' out clothes with you, and hurry up, will ya?"

I nodded and drifted into the constant flow of people clutching bags and going in and out of shops. I felt dirty and didn't want their eyes on me. I entered a store and began weaving in and out of the aisles, apathetic to what I was going to buy. I didn't want to be there. I wandered into another store and thumbed the blouses. What the fuck am I doing? I thought, as my body swayed ever so slightly. I'd had too much drink and not enough coke.

A short brunette girl approached me. "Can I help you find anything?" she asked.

"Dress me," I said.

I walked out of the store fifteen minutes later with two bags of clothes and a double rye and Coke on my mind. Time blurred. I stopped reading my text messages because all of them said the same thing.

You're a fucking loser.
How could you do this?
We are keeping your son. You will never get him back.
Selfish bitch.
The cops are looking for you now. Call home.
Are you okay?
Call home.
Call . . . home.

Each time I read one of the texts, I fell further away from being able to be revived from my walking drug-and-alcohol coma. Delete. Delete. Delete. They only confirmed what I knew: I was fucking hopeless. Now my only task at hand was to forget what a selfish bitch I was so that I could live with myself, which in fact made me a selfish bitch.

We checked in to a hotel room at the Ramada, the same one I had stayed at the year before with my family because I was a creature of habit. The boys went downstairs to have a drink while I got ready. I hopped out of the shower and wrapped the towel around me. My hair was wet. My toes pressed into the linoleum. The mirror was fogged—my reflection was hidden from me just like my emotions. I knew if I allowed myself to feel I would kill myself. I would open the fucking patio door of my seventh-floor hotel room and jump. I clenched my teeth.

Thinking about suicide made me think of my mom.

MOM TAUGHT SUNDAY school when I was a child. When she was around children, she came to life. She created all these interactive songs that would get every six-year-old and their brother hyped on Jesus. We went to church every Sunday in rooms that were swollen with the spirit and full of gospel songs that we sang in Cree. Mom was a proper woman who bent over backward for her kids. She tended gently to other people's children. And those kids flocked to her. Mom had a knack for knowing how to make them feel special. She showed the troublemakers extra attention and an extra dose of gentleness. It made them take a liking to her and they smartened up real quick in her presence. On school trips, Mom always sat with the class outcasts. The ones who were poorer than us and had stringy unwashed hair. I remember being upset about sitting alone in a school bus seat while Mom sat with Gladys and Todd behind me. Mom knew those kids needed some additional love and she didn't let my pouting get in the way of her giving it to them.

When I was in kindergarten, she made me clothes and matching accessories by hand. I was the object of adoration for many years because Mom always went above and beyond when dressing her little princess. Mom grew up poor and she told herself, "No white people will ever look at my children like dirty Indian kids."

Those are good memories.

But the memories of my mom shape-shifted into something else entirely for a period of time.

My first year as a teen and I was enough trouble to have to be shipped away to Prince George. That was also the year my mom started to drink.

I know she spent too many late nights stressing over whether I would be alive in the morning when I took off drinking. She would spend hours combing the streets to find me. She tried to be strong for me and broke under the weight of it all.

When I returned home from Prince George six months later my mom had disappeared.

Instead, I found an angry drunken woman living in her skin.

Us Native women know how to disappear. It's an art, really—we can disappear even when we are right in front of your face. Sometimes on purpose, sometimes out of safety, sometimes by force, and sometimes because we can't see ourselves anymore.

Most of the women in my family have battled with depression. Most of the women in my family have lost this battle at some point in their lives and vanished somewhere deep inside themselves.

This was Mom's era of defeat.

My dad was absolutely consumed by work. His desire to give us what he never had took him completely away from us. Funny how that works. His presence in the household was a rare sight. Mom disappeared and Dad pulled a vanishing act. That separation only deepened the divide between my mother and sobriety. When he was home and she was drunk, which was often, she would follow him around the house screaming obscenities at him.

"Bastard," she would yell. "You're a fuckin' bastard."

My dad would cuss a few times back at her before I would hear the clinking of his keys and the slamming of the front door. I always wondered where he would go. I would wait to hear the door open again and to hear his voice calling us, so we could leave with him. But, he never did come back for us and it always hurt to be abandoned by him and left with my mom. I knew that sometimes he didn't go anywhere. He just slept in the truck in the driveway. Even so, I still wanted him to take us away, even if it was just ten feet outside of the madhouse in which we lived back then.

My littlest brother would always be the one to de-escalate Mom and speak soothing words to her. I disliked her during those moments. It's because I saw so much of myself and my inability to stay sober in her and her life. I think she saw the same in me and she damn well didn't like it either. We were each other's reflection of our own failures. So, when Dad left I became the target of the whisky death machine that controlled her. She would then follow me around the house and call me names until I locked myself in my room or my brother whisked her away.

My struggle wasn't isolated.

I remember staying at a friend's house one time and the same scenario broke out. Her father locked himself in the bathroom and I could hear her mom calling him a bastard while she pounded on the door. We snuck out of the house when they moved the argument downstairs. We put her little brother in the back of my mom's car, which I had borrowed for the night. I was sixteen and finally had some freedom in the form of a licence. We all slept in my bed that night because my home, for once, was actually quiet.

The fighting and yelling seemed like normal behaviour among a lot of the Native friends I had. I didn't have any white friends once I became a teenager, so I didn't know what their homes were like. I had naïvely imagined that their homes were the kind that served cups of hot cocoa on the kind of days when you needed them. Their homes were the kind that had hot water year-round and a working furnace. In these homes they probably had a family game night where the mom made turnovers or popovers, or whatever shit white people make for their kids. The dad would chuckle, "You little rascal," while he messed up his son's hair with his hand. The dad would let his son win the board game. In my mind, white homes had the monopoly on family happiness.

One time I came home from school at lunch to find her drunk and as angry as a woman scorned ten times over. She was eating the hamburgers she had made the night before without a bun, and with the kitchen island between us I was feeling pretty tough.

"Just go to bed," I spat my words at her.

"Don't tell me what the fuck to do! I'm your mother," she yelled as she swayed and took another bite of her hamburger.

"Then act like it," I muttered.

Her eyes went large and she threw the half-eaten hamburger at my head and I had to laugh because a hamburger was being thrown at my head. My laughter set her off. Rage filled her eyes.

"Do you think this is fuckin' funny?" she questioned. Her words were pointed but her legs were wobbly as she moved toward me. I was instantly scared and regretted saying anything.

My mom is not a woman to be fucked with. Drunk or not. She could clean the floor with any man's head if she wanted. I grabbed the house phone off the counter and headed down the hallway. I heard her heavy footsteps coming behind me, so I moved quickly until I reached the bathroom. I locked the door behind me, pulled out all of the drawers in front of the door, and called my dad. She stood on the other side of the door banging on it and taunting me.

"Go ahead, you big fuckin' baby. Call your dad. Cry, cry, cry."

My dad did not answer.

I sat in the bathroom until I couldn't hear her stumbling around the house anymore. Then I made my escape. I walked to my auntie's, the winter air biting my cheeks as tears rolled down.

Liquor seeped into every aspect of our family's lives.

Before Mom started drinking she was damned near a saint. She was a woman devoted to her family who went the extra mile in church and for others. She made the best apple pies for miles in any direction. No one had seen it coming. I guess no one ever does.

My cousin on my dad's side once made the remark, "It's funny how Helen grew up going to church and we didn't. But she's the one who turned out to be the alcoholic."

Estranged cousin irony points: 1.

Another irony? Dad was a preacher on the odd Sunday when there was a vacant pulpit. And if he wasn't at the podium, he would testify to strangers on street corners.

It earned me the nickname "the Rev's Dev," short for the Reverend's Devil.

I was a living oxymoron.

It wasn't the usual case of preacher's daughter gone wild where the daughter was given no trust at all and finally grows a pair and rebels. I was given a lot of trust and I just chose to do shady things. And my mom? Well, her addiction swallowed her and drank her up until she was bone dry. My brothers and I would comb the house for her stash when she was passed out. We'd empty vodka bottles until only an inch of liquor remained and refill them with water.

"You think she'll notice?" my youngest brother would ask nervously.

"Who cares!" my other brother would say as I'd screw the cap back on.

We would hide beer bottles and pray that she thought she drank it all the night before. Not that it mattered because she would just buy more. There was a limitless supply of liquor out there. I learned to hate the sound of clinking beer bottles and the song "Moonlight Eyes," by Nazareth. It meant she was going on a bender.

To this day, there are '80s songs that still trigger me.

Mother eventually became full of her grief. Too full. Her cup runneth over. She became suicidal.

My youngest brother would always try to calm her down and put her to bed. He would find the knife that she'd hidden under her pillow and put it away. Or he would grab the giant plastic bag full of pills she had amassed earlier and place them back in the medicine cabinet. He was a ten-year-old doing palliative care work. He did it all alone. I had my own issues with addiction and my other brother isolated himself.

He would plead with me not to react to her when she was inebriated and angry.

"Please, Helen," he begged, his big brown eyes filled with tears. "Don't say anything back. It'll only make it worse."

Sometimes I would bite my tongue just for him. Other times I would un-rein it and let it lash out at her, which resulted in more yelling and me locking myself in a room with her fists on the other side of the door. Really, though, I was so fucked up. I wanted her to be there for me, but I was never there to protect my brothers. We all absorbed the shocks of her alcoholic tremors in different ways. And when it shook the house, we fell divided.

There would be bouts of sobriety and all would be well in the house. There would be a surplus of money for groceries and Mom would make elaborate meals with desserts prepared from scratch. We ate at the kitchen table like a real family, like we had always done throughout our early childhood. My brothers would be happy, and I would be able to focus a little more clearly at school. We would all quietly wonder if this was a turning point and sometimes we dared to hope it was.

But the dread always crept back in.

The night would take on the ambience that we had just spent the last week trying to forget existed. Music would play, cigarette smoke would waft into our rooms, and she would cry if she couldn't get angry at anyone. Mom cried a lot. I think she just wanted to be loved and to truly love herself. Sometimes an auntie or someone else would come over and eventually they would end up crying together. It was a 3:00 a.m. moonlit family revival where people got redeemed and cried the tears they couldn't acknowledge when they were sober.

I was seventeen when I watched her being wheeled off on a stretcher.

I had to call an ambulance after finding her lying in her bed, more incoherent than usual. I scanned the room and noticed pill bottles that were tipped sideways and lay empty. She had swallowed them all. A rainbow of death. I sat beside her while I screamed for my dad. Her hands felt cold and damp like a winter-kissed window. Her lips blushed blue and grey. She said she could see her uncle who had passed away years before. He wanted her to go with him. Great-Grandpa was there too, she said. She was talking to them.

"I'm ready to leave," she said, her eyes looking past me.

"Mama!" I yelled through my tears as I shook her. "Mama. Stay with me. Stay with me please."

"Uncle. Grandpa."

"Nooooo!" I screamed as I gripped her hand. "No, no, no. Look at me, Mama. Look at me! You need to stay here. Stay with us, Mama."

Her eyes would slowly close and I would shake her till they opened again. Her body was so cold.

"You can't take her. You. Can't." I choked the words out as I held onto my mother and cried. I could barely catch my breath as my anxiety rose higher and higher. It couldn't end like this.

"No, no, no, no . . ." I repeated over and over.

Dad was beside me yelling words at her, trying to get her to stay up. Finally, the medics arrived and I left the room while they hauled her out.

My dad and I stood at the window as the ambulance drove away. The sun was just rising. The world was quiet. And the silence that was left in its wake? It was deafening.

"I don't know what to do anymore," my dad whispered.

That was years ago. And these memories lifted my own fog.

And, as I stared back toward the hotel mirror, I could see myself now. I shook my head. No. I could never commit suicide. I know the mess it leaves behind.

SUICIDE OR NOT, my head still wasn't on right.

I deleted all of the pictures of my son from my cell phone the night I arrived in Edmonton. The photo of us pressing our noses together, smiles stretching outwards and upwards. My heart palpitated. I yearned to be back at that time again. To be sober and strong and present for him. I was meant to be there for him. After all, I dreamt him into existence.

When I was fifteen I dreamt that I gave birth to a brilliantly beautiful boy. My entire being was taken over by a presence of love that I had never known before. The feeling of love was so intense, so real, I can still summon the emotion my body held. In this dream I kept repeating, "I have a son, and his name is Mathias." Just after my twentieth birthday that dream became a reality.

They say that before children come into this world they choose their parents.

He chose me.

I have a son and his name is Mathias.

My people are dreamers. I have dreamer blood in me. My son is living proof.

From the moment he was born, he was loved. I thought I had forgotten how to love entirely until I held him in my arms. The moment he wrapped his tiny delicate fingers around my index finger I was done for. He saved me that time. I became sober and started to put my life back together. I remember his first laugh and how beautiful it sounded. He was lying on the couch with a pillow beside him so he wouldn't roll off. He held the strings to a half-dozen helium balloons that floated overhead. Every time his arm moved, the balloons danced. He gave it a good tug and the balloons moved into each other and scattered about and that was the moment. His little lips parted and he let out the loudest gut-filled laughter. That laugh resonated with my being. That is what a mother's happiness felt like. So much love at once that it pours out of you. I imagine it's like your aura exploding into rainbows.

When I was pregnant with him, I would write him letters in the notebooks I had scattered throughout my room.

Dear Unborn Child,
Don't hate me.

Dear Unborn Child,
I promise to love you. You are loved. I hope that I am
enough for you.

Dear Unborn Child,
It is autumn and the cool air licks my neck. I am at Papa's
and Grandma's for the weekend and I think of you. This process
of preparing for you has left me feeling like a snake that had
to shed its skin. I don't know who I am anymore, but I am
your mother.

I WAS TERRIFIED to become a mother. And even more
terrified of being a horrible drunken mother. I'd seen it
happen. I couldn't stay sober for much longer than a couple
days. But when I found out I was pregnant with him, I
found some strength.

We were inseparable for the entire first year of his life.

My only time away from him happened once a week.

I was volunteering—cooking and serving food at the soup
kitchen in town. I made meals from empty cupboards and
patched together recipes with a bunch of old Catholic ladies.
I loved cooking, serving, and the laughter in the kitchen. I
knew that a very thin line separated me from the homeless
people to whom I served food. I knew that many of them

ended up in the soup lines because of addiction and that I could have been in their place. This knowledge made me put my heart into the food we prepared.

I often thought of my great-uncle. He was homeless too. Every once in a while, one of his old street friends would come over and tell me a story about him.

During that first year with Mathias, Mom was busy raising my new brother. He was only two months older than my son so she was unable to help me much. Both of my parents agreed it would be good to spend that initial year bonding with my baby rather than try to get a job. Time with my son seemed perfect but they say time is money and money was something of which I had very little. My mother told me to apply for social assistance and get on welfare.

But I, the single-mother ex-alcoholic, was too proud to do it. Alcoholic or not, I had worked pretty steady since I was thirteen years old. So I kept my pride, placed it on the kitchen table between my dad and me, and said, "I just don't want to go on welfare, Dad."

He sighed. "I understand, my girl, I was the same way," he said softly. "I can help you so you don't have to, but it won't be much."

We got by on "it won't be much" but we had love.

Love doesn't keep you warm at night, though. I would spend a winter day with my son in our small room that was warmed by the buzzing heater. I had to go as far as placing a towel under the door so the cold wouldn't sneak in and the heat wouldn't creep out. When my son napped in my arms I would stare at him, listen to him breathe. I would tell him about our future together.

"One day, my son," I would whisper to him as I ran my finger over his tiny brow, "one day Mama's going to make a life for us."

That's why I ran away to Edmonton.

I knew I was no longer able to keep that promise.

I had to exist somewhere else. Some place where I couldn't remember him and his smiles or laughter or his love for me. No, that would be too painful. I couldn't live with the memories of having loved so profoundly and abandoning it. I knew the grief would push me over the edge. I wasn't even able to look at any more of the pictures; I just memorized which buttons to press on my cell phone and pressed them.

Delete. Delete. Delete.

It's a scary thing, forcing a part of yourself to die. I was scared of my son seeing me losing all control. I never drank in front of him. I was probably one of the only alcoholics who wouldn't allow drinking in my home when I did have a place of my own. Home was not a place for drinking, it was a place for living, for cooking, for watching movies, and for telling stories. It was where I went over the picture cards I made for us so I could teach him the words in Dane Zaa I was learning from my asu.

Hadaa. *Moose.* Gaa. *Rabbit.* Haklay eenzah. *Moon.* Askae. *Little boy.* Sutzae. *My heart.* Atikae Nochjay. *I love you very much.*

Home. I would never be there again. I was scared I was going to hurt him. Maybe hit him in a drunken stupor or call him names like my mom had called me names when she was still drinking. I was trying to protect him from me.

Disappearing.

That was supposed to be the right thing to do.

MY SECOND NIGHT in Edmonton was strung together by disjointed conversation and straight lines of blow. The morning crept in like an unwanted reminder that the world carried on in spite of our refusal to take part. We ordered food and the boys drank their beers. I drank my rye and Coke. We were in a waiting period.

Waiting for the night.

Darkness was much more accepting of our state. Nothing seemed too shady in the dark. I hit a point where I was stuck inside my head and needed to talk to someone, anyone but Jimmy and Michael. Their conversations went in the same cycles. Camp life at Mile 132 sucking ass. Close encounters with bears, other wildlife, and police officers. Moments in time when they were "The Man." Elaborate plans for projects that would never be attempted. Repeat.

There's always a lot of planning done on drugs, a lot of "high-deas." Once, during a three-day binge elsewhere, a group of us drafted a plan to build a school in Mexico.

"None of that middleman organization shit. If I'm going to do it, I want to do it right," the guy (a.k.a. drug dealer) said as he did a line off the square plate mirror and passed it to his girlfriend.

"No, we could totally go down and get connected. Building permits. Construction crews made up of the locals. All of that," I said.

"Fuck yes. I can bring down a couple guys. Ricky that big bald fuck, he was a carpenter before. Oh and Gary, dude has crazy skills. Crazy," the guy said rapidly and began bouncing up and down in his seat. He bounced when he thought he was making really good recommendations, and sometimes they really were.

Not just planning is done in places like that after two days of no sleep, but a lot of talk about what's needed in the world. We held the capacity to plan at quick cocaine-fueled rates, which sometimes made us feel more genius and capable then we ever were. We could build a school. We could build an off-grid community with a grassroots governing system that also enjoyed the pleasures of heavy cocaine use. We may be derelicts and fuck-ups, but some of us are derelicts with ideals.

Follow-through on drug-den conversations could result in blueprints, masterplans, or patented inventions. "Follow-through" is the key term here.

There were no "high-deas" with Jimmy and Michael, and I was not in the space to try to concoct whimsical plans. I was stuck in my mind. I needed a female to talk to. Besides, I didn't want to talk to Jimmy or Michael about my shit because I thought they might shut the shit show down. I was afraid one of them would say, "Whoa, Helen, that's a little fucked up. Even for us. Let's call it a night."

Then I would have no one to drink into oblivion with.

ANOTHER IMPORTANT RELATIONSHIP in my life was my friend Ellie. Ellie the short-haired Anishinaabe Kwe in Ontario. Her love came without condition. I would call Ellie.

We had spent time together at the national program for Indigenous women in Nova Scotia. Nights under a Mi'kmaw star-scape were spent with bottles of wine and blossomed into drunken philosophy. Drunken philosophy is what we should have gotten a certificate in. Or at least I should have, because Ellie sat with my wild ass while I drank the wine. Ellie had a laugh that carried and was distinguishable from a dozen Indian women's group laughter. When all the bellows melted together and became one, you could still find hers. I called her because she never judged me, not even for a moment—and also because she was halfway across the country and couldn't send someone to come get me. I stood on the patio of our hotel room cradling my rye and Coke. The city lights twinkled in the dark. I could hear a police siren in the distance. I pressed numbers and took a gulp of my drink. The ice cubes clinked against the glass.

"Ellie?"

"That's me," her soft voice answered.

"It's Helen."

"Oh, hey girl!"

"Ellie . . . ," I whispered.

"What's going on?" she asked, her tone changing.

"I'm so fucked up, Ellie. So fucked up and so fucking far gone."

"Okay, whoa, slow it down. What exactly is happening, Helen?"

"I can't fuckin' do it, Ellie. I can't stay sober. There's no point anymore. There's just no point."

"Helen, you're not going to do anything stupid right now are you?"

"Like what?"

"Like, you know . . . kill yourself?"

"No. I'm fuckin' disappearing, man. I left home. I don't know where I'm going . . . but Ellie . . . I wish I could have got it right."

"Where are you?"

"You can't say anything . . ."

"I won't," she promised.

"Edmonton."

"Helen, one thing I know about you is that you are amazing. I know you do a lot of things right. Dude, you should go home."

"No, Ellie . . . ," I said as I turned around with my drink in my hand. "No. You don't know me anymore. I'm different now. I don't know what the fuck I'm doing, Ellie."

"What about your son?"

"I can't . . ." The words cracked as they came out of my mouth.

"Helen, listen—"

"No, Ellie," I cut her off. "I gotta go now. I love you."

I hung up the phone and stared off at the city. It was so busy, so many sounds. So many cars going places. People in their own little lives. So much of everything. I only wanted nothingness.

The patio door slipped open. "Helen, let's roll the fuck out," Jimmy said. "Bar time," he barked.

I slammed the rest of my drink and went back into the hotel room.

"Michael, you going to dance tonight?" I asked as we walked to the elevator.

"You ain't catching me on the dance floor," he answered, his face turning a telling red.

"Nah, not unless they play his song," Jimmy chimed in.

"Oh yeah? What's that? Some Madonna track?" I said, nudging Michael in the arm.

"Pfftt . . . no way." Michael dismissed the comment.

"C'mon, Mikey, sing it with me!" Jimmy yelled.

Jimmy started belting a Hank Williams Jr. track to an unwilling audience. Michael shook his head while Jimmy draped his arm over Michael's shoulder and crooned alone. We hopped in a taxicab and on the way to the bar I caught a glimpse of a woman that looked like Her.

Her. The girl who was my best friend and has always been a thread woven throughout my life and story of survival. I could never escape the thought of Her.

four

I WONDERED IF I WOULD FINALLY SEE HER AGAIN IN these streets. We always gravitated toward each other like two fucked-up magnets with explosives for hearts, hell-bent on uniting and self-destructing.

I remembered us being here, a few blocks away from the same bar we were going to now. This was long before we had children and when we didn't know we were still children ourselves. We were staying at my uncle's apartment on Jasper Avenue, propped up against glass patio doors, our bottoms resting on the cement balcony. I was fifteen years old. Just a kid who thought she knew everything about living. Back then, Edmonton pulsed beneath us, full of what we wanted, but full of even more things we wanted nothing to do with. Our cigarettes dwindled down in complete silence as we watched the smoke travel outwards, upwards, and away.

I had just run away from home again, or maybe it was Her I was running to. I could never figure that out. She used to live a block away from my parents' house. I remember ringing in 1999 by opening my back door at midnight to wave and yell "Happy New Year!" to her across the alleyway as she ran into the driveway and honked the car horn back at me. We screamed New Year's nonsense at each other and laughed. Not long after that, maybe a year or so, is when she moved to Edmonton.

We found each other at the end of grade school, before we were given over to the rapid aging that chased us down in junior high. It was a time when life was a series of check-yes-or-no boxes. We'd pass notes to each other in class.

"Do you like Clinton?" Yes.

"Do you think the new substitute teacher is stupid?" Yes.

There was no heavy playground philosophizing, only matters that were black and white. Yet she and I found shades of grey inside of us that even we didn't know how to communicate. We were two little Native girls, both of us settling into our post-puberty bodies. Both pretty.

But no one told us being pretty and Native was à dangerous combination.

Eventually, we told each other some of the secrets that suffocated us. She started talking about her father's beatings.

I always suspected there was more to her story. She could never fully open. Maybe it hurt too much. We were the same in that way too. I was never open to talking about my sexually warped childhood.

We only had to look in each other's eyes to know that we were both drowning, but in different ways. It didn't need to be said out loud. This knowledge—even through silence—provided a life preserver back then.

We knew without saying. And that's why we loved each other.

We progressed quickly from passing notes to passing cigarettes, bottles, pipes, and lines. We really thought we were fearless as we dived deeper and deeper into the underbelly of addiction.

And Her? She was a scrapper. I remember watching her pummel a girl to her knees in less than a minute.

"Hold my smoke," she said, passing over a newly lit cigarette.

Before the smoke was done the girl she fought was sprawled out on the ground in front of our junior high.

"What did you do that for?" I asked.

"She looked at me funny," she answered, shrugging her shoulders as I passed her the still-lit cigarette.

I admired that about Her. She dealt with her issues through fighting while I resorted to crying. She was a tough girl who would lip-synch with me at sleepovers but still insist on doing the breakfast dishes. One time, I headbutted her while I was drunk. Mom and Dad had tracked us down and were trying to take us home. She was willing to listen while drunk me blatantly refused and tried to pull a less-than-graceful escape. She tried to help them rein me in and I smashed my head into her face. The next day she told me "I love you" through a busted lip.

She was loyal like that. We were all too understanding of each other's dysfunction.

We promised each other that our first-born girls would hold the other's name as their middle name. Correction—we pinky-promised on that shit.

There is a little girl out there somewhere with my name.

I met her once but I was still too young and too drunk to have actually been worthy of her having my name.

The Baby Daddy was always trying to get Her to settle down but she would not be tamed.

The third or fourth time I ran away to Her, before the baby, is when we were staying not far from here. It was a time that would always weigh heavy on me.

We'd gone back inside my uncle's apartment when her phone buzzed. It was him. We'd been out all afternoon window-shopping on Whyte Avenue, looking at things neither of us could afford. We were mid-stride and actively dreaming when he said hello. He was way too old for us. He had on expensive clothes, drove a nice car, and insisted on taking us for lunch. We hopped on a free lunch and went with him. We sat in an Italian restaurant and as I flipped through the menu, I remembered being at that same restaurant before—with my family.

My father had ordered us escargot because he thought it was necessary that we tried everything at least once. He always tried to give us—his children—the experiences that he never had. This included escargot.

I'm pretty sure the experiences he wanted for us didn't include free lunches with creepy old men. A girl's gotta eat and there is always some weirdo pervert willing to play Daddy.

The man was Persian and talked a lot without saying much. His cologne wafted over the table at us as he talked at us, his voice thick with an accent. He wore his hair close to bald, had a nose that was just slightly too large for his face, and rocked a V-neck shirt with a tuft of hair peeking up from the collar. He wasn't a handsome man. I wouldn't say that he was ugly, either, but it was obvious we were both too young and too pretty to be hanging out with the likes of him. He asked us how old we were.

Fifteen.

We didn't ask about his age.

He told us we were pretty.

A danger signal. A red flag.

We had learned by that time that being pretty and Native was a dangerous thing.

After we finished lunch, he got her number and dropped us off close to my uncle's. He texted us. Of course he texted us. He was old and the lunch was just a pre-predatory move. We both wanted to do some drugs and drink our way into a stupor but we had no money. We told him that. He said he would pay three hundred dollars for me to take a ride alone with him. I wasn't so naïve. I knew that the ride would end with him wanting to fuck in his back seat.

"I'll do it," I said.

"No," she replied. "It changes you. Trust me. I have done it already so I can do it."

"Men have always taken it from me for free when I'm drunk. This will be just like that. I might as well get some money," I said, trying to act brave.

"No, Helen. Fuck that. I am going to tell him to come pick me up and when he does I will send you his licence plate number."

The first time she had pulled a trick was when she was fourteen. I remember hearing the story and wanting to be able to be together and protect each other.

I didn't reply to her suggesting I copy his plate number.

I said nothing.

I didn't want to be like all the people who have used her. I wasn't any of the men in her life that continually circled her like scavengers. They took turns picking her bones clean. The world had already feasted on the best parts of me. I understood what it was like to be taken, to be used, to be discarded.

I wanted to tell her to forget about it. I wanted to say that there was nothing wrong with staying sober for one night. We could play the radio and lip-synch like we were twelve again. I wanted to say fuck that creepy old-balls man and his three hundred dollars. We didn't need that. I wanted to tell her that she was much too valuable for a price tag to be put on her. I wanted to hug her until my own swirling madness and addiction stopped and I could see clearly. But I didn't. My monster outweighed my heart.

I wanted to get drunk and high.

She put on her jacket and closed the door.

Thirty minutes later I heard a knock at the door. I opened it to find Her on the other side laughing.

"The fucking elevator broke down!" she howled.

"What?" I said, and I started to laugh too.

"The elevator broke down with me in it," she said, "and I was stuck in it this whole time. So by the time I got down there he was already gone."

We both burst into laughter and shook our heads. Our ill intentions got shuffled away for the night and I made us something for dinner from the almost empty cupboards. We sat at the table, each not acknowledging our urges to get blitzed. We ate our food.

In the quiet space of us falling asleep I heard it: the "no" that I should have said.

I only saw Her a few more times after that night.

So here I am again in this city that holds so many memories of Her and the fucked-up things we did when we thought we knew what we were doing.

I'd put out the call but nothing came back and I could hear the emptiness echo.

Maybe I would see Her.

I stared out at the passing city scenery.

And somewhere out there . . . is a little girl with my name.

"HELEN," MICHAEL SAID. "Helen, snap out of it." He pushed my shoulder.

I looked at him blankly.

"We're here."

I had nodded off in the cab on our way to the bar. I snapped out of it.

I resumed my faux role of being in charge. Of whom? Certainly not myself.

"Well, why are you standing there still? Go get me a drink!" I said, half joking, as I crawled out of the vehicle.

Michael ushered me inside and up to the bar, where Jimmy was sitting, already holding a Budweiser. There weren't a lot of people at this bar and I was fine with that. I didn't really feel like meeting new people.

"Game of pool?" Michael asked me.

I shook my head and nodded toward Jimmy. I sat on the stool and took off my brown fake-leather jacket. The stool wobbled. Or maybe I wobbled.

"Double rye and Coke," I said to the blond behind the counter.

I watched him tend to the alchemy of bartending, his muscled frame apparent under his white T-shirt. If I wasn't so fucked up, I'd hit on that, I thought.

"You're gorgeous," I blurted out when he gave me my drink.

Apparently, I was fucked up enough to not care about being fucked up.

He laughed and uttered a thank you. His blue eyes were piercing.

"You with them?" he said as he nodded toward the boys.

Jimmy was busy strumming on his pool stick like he was ripping on a guitar. Michael was egging him on, making Slayer signs at him and nodding his head.

"Yup, but not 'with them,' though," I said, making air quotations with my fingers. "They're old friends from way back."

"So are you 'with' anybody?" he asked me, mirroring my air quotations.

Then it swept in slowly, like the sun creeping up on the back of my neck. Anxiety.

He must have known I hadn't slept in two days. He must. Anything that I was about to say was going to let him know that I've been up and on drugs. Fuck. Try to act normal.

"No," I said, as I took a deep drink.

The handsome bartender, of course, wasn't drinking. He was on the clock. Fuck me, I thought. He knows for sure. This must be some kind of weird game. Why does he want to know if I'm single? He must be fucking with me. What a dickhead.

"I gotta go," I said as I stood abruptly and walked toward the boys.

"Guys," I said shakily.

It felt like everyone in the bar was watching me. Do they all know? They are just waiting for me to do some weird tweaker shit. Fuckers.

"I need to go,"

"Aw, we just got here," whined Jimmy.

"I don't mind going," said Michael.

He looked at me eagerly. Maybe he thought this was his opportunity.

"No," I said, "You stay with Jimmy. But before I go I need to get some more shit."

"Oh fuck, that's right," Jimmy said, slamming his hand to head.

"Yeah, that's fucking right," I repeated to him, rolling my eyes.

"Well, uh, Michael," Jimmy said, "call your friend."

MICHAEL'S FRIEND SHOWED up twenty minutes later. His tall Cree frame sauntered slowly into the room. He scanned the bar when he walked in—as if he was taking a mental inventory of potential witnesses.

The friend reminded me of one of the first people I smoked crack with. I didn't like him. He talked in such a way that you knew he would eventually fuck you over. It wasn't in the words, either. It was the way that he said it. I've done drugs with enough characters that I can tell a shady one when I do drugs with them.

"Two grams," I whispered to Michael and slid the money into his pocket.

I wasn't dealing with this guy if I didn't have to.

They disappeared into the bathroom together.

I sat on the wooden stool, my elbow propped on the narrow wooden counter by the pool table. I stared blankly at the television mounted in the corner. It was flashing sports highlights. My anxiety had subsided and the bartender was looking gorgeous again.

I never understood the anxiety that would overwhelm me out of nowhere. I used to get really bad panic attacks. So, this drug- and sleep-deprivation-induced mini episode was nothing in comparison. Once, after a night of drinking, I was sitting on my friend's porch in the summer's heat wearing a pink cowboy hat and biting my tongue so I wouldn't choke on it. During these attacks it was as if my tongue was going to slither into the back of my throat like a snake in reverse and be the death of me. I would get this overwhelming feeling that nothing in the world was right, and nothing would ever be right. It was in those moments I was at the highest risk of suicide. I could never find the words to formulate the feelings. Instead I would literally bite my tongue.

Michael finally emerged from the bathroom. Alone. I notice him sniffling. Bastard was doing lines without me.

"He wants another twenty bucks for delivery," he said.

"Fuck him," I said, but I reached for my wallet at the same time.

I had no inclination to wander the streets to find another connection. I put another bill in Michael's hand. He held on to my hand a few seconds too long and gave it a squeeze. I rubbed my hand on my jeans—like we were thirteen again and Michael had cooties.

"Check this shot out," Jimmy said as he cracked the cue and sank a striped ball. He was content at the pool table. I almost forgot he was there. My eyes kept flitting from the bathroom to the TV, where an Oilers game was playing. From the bathroom—to the TV.

Jimmy raised his hands above his head, he was pleased with himself.

"Bet you can't do it again," I said.

"Bet what?" he said smartly, with a wink.

"Yeah, right," I snorted, "I'll bet you a shot of tequila."

"How about if I get it in we both take a shot. And if I don't get it in . . . we both take a shot?"

"Deal."

He sinks the shot. We both take a shot. Michael and his cousin join us at the bar and order a shot for themselves. I stared at Michael like a lost puppy dog. I was a lost puppy who needed to snort a line of cocaine to find its way home. Or to forget the way home. Michael stood beside me and grabbed my hand. I felt the plastic baggie. I smiled. I placed the baggie in my pocket, pulled a straw from the bar as discreetly as I could. I walked into the washroom and directly into one of the sickly-orange-painted stalls. If vomit were orange, it would be this hue. I wiped the back of the toilet lid with a tissue then emptied a little of the white messiah onto it. The stall was classically scribbled on.

For free moustache rides call . . .
Rachel wuz here

Daniel Goverbaum likes it in the bum!
Never give up

My eyes lingered on "Never give up." The saying irritated me violently. *What the fuck did that fuck know about reality?* I thought angrily to myself as I fished out my driver's licence and began to crush and cut up my lines. I pulled the red straw from my pocket and fetched my nail clippers from my purse and snipped it to the size of my pinkie.

Never give up. *Pffft.*

I used to think that. I used to preach that.

And look at me now.

I needed oblivion. I needed it now. I needed it yesterday. I would need it tomorrow and the day after that. I inhaled a line, pinched my nostrils twice, then snorted back the second. I flushed the toilet out of habit and exited the orange-vomit stalls.

The boys cranked their heads back at me as I approached. Michael's friend had started a conversation with a tall blonde standing beside him. He looked predatory.

"I'm still outtie, boys."

"What? Why?" Michael whined.

"An empty hotel room with a big bed and a fridge full of booze, that's why."

"Fine," Michael replied.

"A big bed, eh? I know what you're going to get up to by yourself," Jimmy said, nodding in my direction.

"Fuck off," I bit back.

"Only kidding," he said, his arms raised as if to show he meant no harm.

I called a cab and went outside to smoke and wait. I was halfway through my smoke when the door creaked open and Michael trailed outside.

Fuck.

"I'm coming with you," he stated.

There was no room in the silence for a refusal. I nodded my head and passed him my lit cigarette. He took a drag. We said nothing until the cab arrived. When we got into the cab my phone buzzed. I hesitantly looked down at it, ready to shove it back into my pocket if it was another message from my family.

Hey Helen where r u

It was Alex.
I texted him back.

In your city. What the fuck is up?

Busy tonight but will c u tomorrow if u r still here
I will be

Kk, can't wait to c u!

I met Alex at a bar a few years ago. Back when I was sober. Sober, even in bars. I remember seeing his tall, lean frame and messy blond hair bobbing to the music. He was wearing a T-shirt from a punk band I used to listen to and it was enough common ground to spark up a conversation.

"NOFX?" I said, nodding toward his shirt. I loved that band.

Alex threw up the Slayer sign. "Fuck yes."

We went for breakfast the following morning and he invited me to come to Edmonton to a Dropkick Murphys concert with him. It was a month away. Even though I barely knew him, I agreed and ended up in a sweaty mosh pit crashing into shirtless sweaty men who probably got more out of pushing people than the music. I didn't drink a drop back then, but Alex smoked weed and drank. I let him know that I wasn't looking to start something with someone who wasn't sober so we respected our differences and stayed friends. Whenever he would pass through town I would cook a hot meal for him and we would catch up over my wooden table. Alex was always kind and soft-hearted to me but also able to joke around about the dark stuff in life that you needed to poke fun at. He was a good guy but I would never allow for our relationship to change from a friendship. I was what another man had referred to as a "five-star woman." The one you settle down with and marry. I was the elusive woman back then.

Now?

The not-so-elusive woman on drugs.

Alex no longer knew me.

AFTER READING THAT text, I watched the city lights pass by as we zigzagged through the streets, making our way back to the hotel.

"Are you okay?" Michael asked.

"Yeah. I'm good," I answered.

I stayed facing the window until we arrived at the hotel. I knew that if I looked at Michael now I would fall apart. I had no room for emotions where I was headed. They would open up wounds and be the death of me. I knew that Michael cared about me and part of the reason for him coming to Edmonton was probably to make sure I would be okay. I caught him watching me with a look of concern a few times. When he knew I'd deciphered his facial expression, he would turn away and take a drink of his beer.

I didn't want to be worried about.

Not here.

Not like this.

Not by him.

When we got to the hotel room, I put on my faux face again. "Change the channel," I said as I cut up a line on the desk.

"Whatcha wanna watch?" Michael asked.

"Anything but this shit. I hate reality TV shows. Nothing real about them."

"You got it, boss," he said, flicking through the channels and stopping on an old horror movie.

"Not this either."

"Ha ha, well, fuck," he said, tossing the remote across the bed. "You pick then."

"Geez, Mikey, even half-assing changing the channel."

"Half-ass? I never half-ass nuthin."

"So what are ya saying? You only full-ass it?"

"That's right, I put my whole ass into it," he said, laughing.

"Hey, Michael?"

"Yeah?"

"Does that make you an ass-whole?"

Michael and I busted our guts laughing.

"Get the fuck outta here and choose your damn show!" he howled.

I snorted the line. My nose was reaching the point where it felt constantly plugged and lines were getting harder and harder to get through it. I pushed my finger up against my nostril and snorted air back twice for good measure. At this stage, the stage of drug-ate-up nostrils, it always felt like the drugs weren't making it to where they were supposed to.

We sat and drank and watched two episodes of *The Millionaire Matchmaker*. Yes, I made Michael watch *The Millionaire Matchmaker*, a reality show I actually liked because it was fascinating. We sat there high and drunk waiting to see if Thomas the multi-millionaire would choose his trademark busty brunette or actually go for a woman he had a future with. I knew this show wasn't about love but it made me think of the chance of love.

I would never have that.

Ever since that fucking incident.

I wasn't able to give voice to the story yet. I could feel its memory thrash about inside my skin.

Love . . . will never be mine.

I felt empty and hollow when I thought about love. A tree that has lost its insides, with its roots slowly decaying beneath. I was just waiting for the fall all this time.

After the last episode of *The Millionaire Matchmaker* wrapped up, I tossed the remote at Michael.

"About time," he said. "Won't let me watch a scary movie but will make me watch a show about gold diggers."

"Gold diggers need love too, Michael," I retorted while laughing.

"And what about me?"

"What about you?"

"Don't I need love too?"

I didn't know what to say to him. But thankfully—just as the silence got awkward—Jimmy walked in with the untrustworthy friend, another guy, and two girls trailing in behind him. Great, I thought. Now I'll be expected to be capable of conversation.

"What are you lame asses doing anyways? Any fuckin' happening in here?" the friend said.

Classy fucking men emerge in this lifestyle.

"No," I replied, "no fucking happened in here—and the chances of any fucking went down a hell of a lot as soon as you walked in."

Everybody laughed but the friend. He shot me a steely look. I didn't trust him. Just having him in the room raised my guard. I would need more cocaine—if only to suffer through this intrusion.

I cut up another line while everyone figured out what they wanted to drink.

"I'll have a beer," the new guy said. I hadn't seen him earlier at the bar. He was tall, white, with big shoulders and blue eyes. He was good-looking in spite of the small pock marks on his cheeks.

"Do you have any coolers?" the blonde girl asked. She was the one the cousin had picked up earlier at the bar.

I rolled my eyes. Coolers? What a fucking joke, I thought.

"Only hard liquor and booze around here, sweetie," Jimmy called out to her from the mini-fridge.

"Got any vodka?" the blonde's friend asked. She wasn't as pretty as her friend, but had big boobs and nice brown hair.

"Vodka we got!" Jimmy said victoriously.

"I'll have that too, with pineapple and Seven-Up," the blonde piped up.

"Vodka and Sprite it is," Jimmy said. He began to pour them drinks. The girls laughed.

I looked at the tall white guy. "What's your name?" I asked, nodding in his direction.

"Billy," he answered while taking a step toward me and extending his hand.

"Helen," I responded. We shook hands.

I sat there, floating in and out of conversation, letting them talk and interjecting a couple lines of my own here and there. I felt awkward and clumsy. I knew if I started talking I wouldn't shut the fuck up.

I watched more than I listened. The friend made sure the blonde didn't get too far away from him. If she got up and danced, he stood up and lurked. Billy played old rap music on his phone and bullshitted with Michael. Jimmy was trying hard to move in on the busty brunette. The brunette liked fucking with Jimmy's brain. Teasing. She would let him grab her ass before pushing him away. The blonde cuddled in close to the cousin when he would take out more cocaine. I emptied out the last of my baggie and snorted it, licked my finger and picked up what was left. I rubbed it over my teeth.

Numbness. Fucking numbness.

Every now and again, I would realize that I wasn't supposed to be where I was.

I should have been at home. I should have been at home and next to my son in bed. I should have told my baby a bedtime story using the Dane Zaa language for the names of the animals and rivers. I crafted stories for him with Askae and Asu as the central characters.

That's what I should have been doing. I should have been at home like a real mother is supposed to be.

The anxiety, panic, and fear rushed up from my chest again and into my throat. I struggled to breathe.

I got up and went out onto the patio. I gripped the railing and took a deep breath. The chatter in my mind started up and so many voices were going at once. Tears welled in my eyes. One voice said, "Nothing will ever be the same again." Another said, "Die to what you know. It's the only way." I clenched the railing and shook it ferociously. I was a caged animal inside of my body. The glass door slid open. I gritted my teeth, clenched my jaw, and blinked my tears back, then took another deep breath.

"You having a smoke?" Billy said as he came up behind me. Smooth Moves McGee placed his hand on my lower back.

"Yeah, I was about to," I said as I stepped back from him and sat in the plastic armchair.

Laughter erupted from inside the room. I lit my cigarette. Billy sparked his.

"You know you're sexy as fuck, right?" he said to me with a twinkle in his eyes.

"You think so, eh?" I said. I wasn't in the mood for bullshit.

"Yeah, girl, you know. As soon as I walked in I was like, damn, I want to know that girl."

I laughed.

"What? You think that's funny?"

"You just want to fuck me."

"No. Damn, girl. All I said is I want to know you. Ain't nobody said nothin' about fuckin'."

"Knowing. Fucking. What's the difference?"

"Shoot, you're a tough girl, ain't ya?"

"I've just known too many guys who wanted to fuck me—or, wait, who wanted to get to know me."

"Well, I ain't like that. Come here," he said as he grabbed my hand and pulled me off the chair.

He pulled me in close and looked at me with his big blue eyes.

You're just like that, I thought right before I let him kiss me. I already knew the game beforehand. I was well versed in false sincerity, lacklustre eye twinkles, and forgetful fingers.

When I was thirteen, I fell prey to empty confessions of "like" and ended up feeling broken by the callousness of boys. It didn't help that with my history of childhood sexual abuse, I started out of the gates equating sex with love. We shag and this means you love me, right? Wrong.

Eventually, I became spiteful and would use up men as if it was my great retribution. I hurt you like I was hurt and I feel better about myself in the end, right? Wrong again.

Some were good men. Some were nice men. Some were broken like me and we cut each other with our jagged edges. I vanished from beds before the morning sun arose. I lied about like. I held tarnished stars in my eyes. I did fucked-up things. I hurt people. I pretended I wasn't hurting.

I played this game, like Billy is doing now.

I let Billy slide his hand down to my ass. It made me feel like less of a monster to touch another human being. I needed to feel human.

"Come with me to the lobby," I said as I pulled my lips back from his.

"For what?"

"I gotta get money out," I answered. There was no way I was going to be a cocaine bunny and snuggle in close to that creep of a friend to get free blow. I'd rather buy my own shit this time while I still had the money to do so. Maybe Billy would get to "know" me, and maybe I could stay with him for a few days until I figured shit out.

But he would expect sex and I couldn't do that.

"Where you guys going?" the blonde asked as we opened the room door.

"Cash money," Billy said as he rubbed his fingers together.

We got in the elevator and Billy cornered me in it. He kissed my neck and put his hungry hands on my ass. He was a good kisser and I kissed him back like I meant it.

"Damn, girl," he said as he grabbed my hand and pulled me out of the elevator.

We got to the ATM and he pulled me to him and kissed me again.

"I got this, girl," he said as he pulled out his wallet.

I was going to stop him and then thought better of it.

"How much should I take out?"

I shrugged.

"Aight, I'll take out two bills," he said.

When men "got your back" like this, you know you have to make them feel special. You have to be sexy and flirty and fluff their ego. It's a part of the game.

Billy put the cash in his wallet and turned to me almost expectantly. He was my knight riding in high on a pony called Cocaine. I moved forward and threw my arms around his neck. I kissed him hard but pulled back just as quickly.

"Let's go," I said grabbing his hand and leading him back toward the elevator.

Billy bought us more drugs. I grabbed him a beer and myself a rye and Coke. I waited expectantly for him to bust some lines on the desk but he motioned for me to follow him to the bathroom.

Fuck! I cringed inside.

I walked into the bathroom and before I could shut the door he grabbed me by my ass and pulled me into him.

"Easy, cowboy," I said, pushing him gently back.

"I can't help it, girl. You're just so fuckin' sexy."

"Just in a rush to know me, eh?"

He shot me a serious look.

"Sorry, couldn't help it." I kissed him quickly on the lips. "Well, what are you waiting for?"

"You want the D?" he said, pointing at his pants.

"Fuck—the coke, Billy. The coke."

"I know, I know," he said, laughing as he pulled out the baggie.

He cut three big lines up. We each did one and split the last one. I looked at myself in the mirror. I didn't even feel real anymore.

What the fuck am I doing here with this fucking clown, I thought.

Billy stood behind me and pulled my ass hard into his crotch. I stood up against him, trying to move my ass away.

He grabbed my breast and pulled me back against him. He leaned his head down to mine and whispered, "I want to fuck you so hard right now."

I turned around and kissed him. Sometimes the best way to forget that some messed-up event is actually your reality is just to go with it. To get it over with. It's too hard to fight it.

I have learned that my whole life.

He lifted me up onto the counter and began to kiss me fast and sloppily. He reached to unbutton my pants and I pushed his hand away. He reached again. I pushed away again.

"Damn, girl, what the fuck?"

My anxiety crept in.

I hadn't had sex since that night.

The night I still couldn't talk about.

I didn't lose my life—but I lost something. I lost things I didn't know how to articulate. Billy's hands unearthed those bones.

"I can't!" I shoved him so hard that he almost lost his balance. I left the bathroom.

Billy followed me out and sat beside me on the bed. He tried to put his hand on my lap but I pushed it off. I felt dirty again. I didn't want to be touched. It made me think of what had happened. I was fucked for the rest of my life. Eventually the two girls left with the friend, Jimmy passed out, Michael fell asleep in the chair, and Billy was still up with me but had stopped trying to put his hands on me.

By this time, it was already late afternoon.

"What happened? Like, we was all cool then you just flipped a switch?" he asked.

"I don't want to talk about it. It's not you. Just some shit, okay. Drop it."

"Fine then, that's cool. We don't have to fuck. Just let me kiss you," Billy said. He moved in close one more time.

I let him kiss me but felt my body clench and tighten. I was too aware of how much I didn't want to do this. My skin crawling. I pulled back again.

"I need another drink," I said.

Billy went to the mini-fridge.

"You got beer and fireball left."

"Beer," I said.

He cracked the can and passed it to me. I drank it fast.

"Whoa, slow down, girl."

"I'm not a girl," I said as I gulped back the rest. "Now pass me another one."

"Whatever you say," Billy said, and he reached into the fridge again.

I took a small sip this time.

"Okay," I said. "You can kiss me now."

He kissed me, I kissed back. He pushed himself into me. We stopped every now and again to cut up a line or go for a smoke. He didn't reach for my pants again.

I was grateful.

My phone buzzed. Again, it was Alex.

Where r u?

Come see me!

Where

Ramada. Rm 617

B there in a few hours k

Ok :)

"Fuck," I said.
"What?" Billy asked.
"I gotta shower and change."
"Can I come?"
"Pfttt . . . no, Billy. You can't."
I dug into my plastic shopping bags and selected an outfit. Alex would make me feel like a human. And spending time with him would remind me that I was.

BY THE TIME I finished getting ready, the boys were up again. We ordered pizza. They cracked beers within twenty minutes of waking up, probably more to ward off a hangover and less because they actually wanted to. Billy left while I was in the shower. I felt relieved, but the asshole didn't even leave a phone number before he left. That's how much he wanted to know me and not fuck me.

"Did you sleep?" Michael asked me.

I shot him an annoyed look. "You my mama now?"

"Just wonderin'," he said.

"We're almost out of booze, guys," I said, doing a shitty job of hiding the panic in my voice.

"Find a delivery service. I ain't moving for shit," Jimmy croaked.

I pulled out the phone book but it was hard to focus. The letters and words were all jumbled together and my mind couldn't crack the code of basic spelling and alphabetical order. I flipped back and forth between pages before I tossed the phone book to Michael. He ordered us a thirty-pack of beer. I wanted him to order some hard liquor too. I was anxious that he was only going to get a thirty-pack and it would not be enough. The worst thing is running out. I reminded him it was nighttime and the liquor stores were going to close soon.

He just stared at me blankly.

"More, Michael," I said, "you gotta order more."

My chest burned from all the anxious energy bouncing around in my body. I knew I would have to sleep soon but sleeping meant waking up, possibly sober. Sober meant reality. Reality was that I had left my child eight hours away. Reality was that I couldn't get it together. Reality was that I was a riddled-up mess with a death wish. I would never fucking escape this darkness.

"Die to God and let God die to you," the darkness whispered.

The darkness was right.

I HAD MADE several previous attempts at sobriety and achieving some level of normalcy, but freedom always eluded me. The first time I went to a treatment centre I was four-teen years old. It was just after my second run away from home—to Her in Edmonton.

The youth rehab I went to was one I would become familiar with over the years. It was a twenty-eight-day program in Prince George, four hours and mountains away from home. My parents were stern and told me that I could either go to treatment or go into foster care.

I reluctantly went into treatment.

The centre was in a side-building off the hospital. Its rooms attempted to be homey but still felt institutional. The pale green walls seemed to be closing in on me as soon as I arrived. I sat across from one of the workers, who was going through my belongings looking for drugs. He confiscated my razors in case I was at risk for suicide. He also took my shaving cream and hairspray, which was bizarre to me. It was later I learned that he took it so I couldn't do "whip-its." Apparently, tilting an empty aerosol can and spraying air into your mouth gets you high and feeling funny. I noted this—just in case I ever had an empty can of whip cream and wanted to give'r a go.

I cried myself to sleep that first night. I was quiet though, so the girls in the rooms on either side of me wouldn't hear my weeping and think I was a bitch. It wasn't my choice to be there and I engaged with the workers with resistance and teenage angst. But there was a boy there whose presence softened me. He was the first long-haired Native boy I had ever met. He wore his hair back in a braid. This boy could sing hand drum songs with perfect pitch. I didn't know any boys who sang any kind of songs like that. He could shoot hoops against the six-foot-four counsellor and win. I found out that his mother had committed suicide a few years before, and my broken spirit wanted to love his broken spirit. I thought he was so beautiful. However, he wanted to love the big-breasted white girl who loved meth. I was okay with admiring him from afar. Being around him made my dislike of hospital food, early nights, and monitored TV time easier to bear.

I completed the program in just a few weeks and stayed clean for a few weeks more. Then I was back on the bottle.

Within a year of drinking, new monsters showed up. I started smoking crack during another run away to Her.

She picked me up at the Greyhound in Edmonton with a couple of older Indians; one of the guys was an older predatory drug dealer. We went to some shady basement apartment. We sat on stools as they pulled out the plastic baggies. She tapped a long cigarette ash onto tinfoil attached to some homemade smoking contraption. The next thing I knew, lighters were being sparked. This was my first crash course in smoking crack. The plastic bottle filled up with smoke and I watched Her suck slowly before she put her lips near mine. She blew the smoke into my mouth to give me seconds.

"It's not the same as smoking weed, Helen. You gotta go a little slower and suck a little lighter," she said. "Now you try it."

I could feel the lightness of the smoke slowly filling up my lungs for the first time. It was when I exhaled that I became infatuated. Whenever we smoked crack, I wanted more. If we weren't smoking, I was fine without it. But as soon as that smoke passed my lips a switch flipped. I became a bottomless crack-smoking pit.

One time I was smoking with the boys back home and there were some older, shadier guys at the house. All the boys we rolled with were rough around the edges. Some came from broken homes with even rougher edges. Whenever there were older men around, I knew not to upset them and definitely not to trust them.

"You got any more?" I asked one of the older guys after I'd smoked the pipe dry.

"Depends," he said through his accordion teeth and pock-marked brown skin.

"Depends on what?" I asked.

We were sitting in the room alone. Everyone else was drinking in the kitchen. Tupac's "Hail Mary" streamed in from the crack between the door and the frame. I felt naked sitting there on that bed with that old man leering at me. He must have been close to forty years old. I had just turned fifteen.

"What are you going to give me for it?" he answered, his eyes flicking back and forth over my body.

I wanted to tell him to fuck off. But I wanted the pipe to be filled up again too.

"What do you want?" I asked, looking away from him. I stared at some of the random garbage on the ground.

"I want to fuck you," he said. His voice raspy and eager.

I stayed facing the ground, "How much will that get me?"

"Sixty bucks' worth."

"Are you fuckin' kidding me?" My eyes snapped upwards. "I want at least two hundred dollars' worth."

"No. Sixty bucks' worth is all I'll give you," he said gruffly, his eyes still stuck on my exposed skin.

"You're fucking crazy, old man," I said as I reached for my beer and got off the bare mattress we were sitting on. I went to leave the room.

He grabbed me by the wrist hard and jerked me back toward the bed. "Where do you think you're going?" he growled.

"Let go of my hand, you're hurting me."

"I'm not letting go of nothing," he said as he yanked me toward him.

At that moment, my friend Jay walked in. He saw the old man's hand around my wrist. Jay's expression made it look like his eyes were going to explode out of his head.

"WHAT THE FUCK ARE YOU DOING?!" Jay screamed, his shoulders up, arms out, and muscles tensed.

"Nothing man, nothing at all. Just chill, little brother. Chill." The old guy released my wrist. He moved back toward the wall. Jay barked at me to get out of the room.

As I scurried out, I heard something smash behind me. Jay came out a few minutes later.

I didn't ask if it was the guy's head that he smashed or if it was something else.

Before I could escape that year, I found myself lost in crack. I also started drinking even more heavily than before. It landed me in treatment again.

I didn't cry that time around. I remember the first night just staring up at the ceiling and wondering if I would get it right this time. The routine was the same as the last time: Eat, morning group, school, exercise, dinner, group, sleep. Repeat.

Twice a week, we went to an Alcoholics Anonymous group and listened to the stories of other people. They were struggling in the middle of their addiction or they spoke from the opposite end of a sturdy sobriety. No one from our group ever talked. We sat on the sidelines and witnessed others who sometimes felt it was their chance to scare us straight. They'd tell us their grimiest rock bottom stories. I don't think any of us batted an eyelash.

Bring it, AA is what our faces said. *Hit us with your most fucked-up childhood and blackout story, we have heard it all.*

I started drinking coffee in AA. Black coffee. I drank it even though it tasted like shit and upset my stomach. It seemed like the AA thing to do. All the other alcoholics gave up drink for low-budget coffee. I drank it black because it was strong and bitter and mildly reminded me of having to drink liquor straight from the bottle.

One thing that did change at the treatment centre was that we were no longer allowed to smoke. The first time, we had a ten-cigarette-a-day allowance. I would trade extra cigarettes for things like contraband chocolate bars or choice of television show when we had TV time. This time, there was no cigarette allowance and this angered many of our inner nicotine fiends.

Two of us devised a remedy to this collective malaise.

A blonde meth addict named Ashley and I figured out that we could bum a smoke from someone at AA. Later, we looked for the best spot to smoke without getting caught. We settled for the top floor of a building that was being renovated. We would excuse ourselves at different times and meet upstairs. We would use the element from the stove to light our smoke and dash out onto the deck. Our plan went perfectly and we laughed at our ability to mastermind a nicotine fix. But when we reached the main floor of our residence, we knew we were caught.

We were met by one of the counsellors. His big arms were folded. His brow was creased, and we were screwed. "Ladies," he said, "time to pack your bags." That was how I failed to stay sober after my second time in treatment. I took it as a sign.

I was blacked out within a week of my discharge, but I did stay away from crack this time around.

Avoiding crack points: 1.

The third time I went to treatment I completed it and some shit actually stuck to the wall of my brain. I made my first real attempt to stay sober afterwards. When I returned home, I found my bedroom transformed. My auntie and my mom bought me new African safari–print bedding, bought me a TV, and placed small elephant figurines around the room.

"A new beginning," Mom said happily, as she showed me my new room and plopped herself on my bed.

"You can do this, my girl," said my auntie.

I cried. Partially because I was happy that they would do this for me. Partially because I was terrified I was going to let them down. I wanted so desperately to become the daughter and person they sometimes still saw in me. I wanted to feel like I wasn't the family fuck-up and constant disappointment.

I went to school and I studied hard. I stopped hanging out with most of my friends, but eventually, life as a sober single teenager got lonely. I stayed sober for four months before I drank myself into a blackened thundercloud.

My addiction was in charge again. It told me that it would strike when it pleased, regardless of how much I wanted it to leave me alone.

After this I plunged myself further and further into being wasted. I would cut class and wander around drunk, trying random drugs that my friend would steal from her uncle. I tried meth for the first time. It took me to another plane of reality. I dropped E. That ecstasy lived up to its name. I swallowed mysterious pills. I kept snorting coke.

All this drug use caused me to pass out once in public. It happened on a city bus in the middle of the day. My father pulled some insane Sherlock moves and found me. He flagged down the bus to haul his comatose daughter off it. It must have been a really tough time for Dad, because during this period my mom was in the thick of her addiction too. It was next-level mom and daughter drama.

I would sit in Comparative Civilizations class, listening to the teacher talking about the Bedouin people, and all I could think about was how my brothers and I had sat in the hallway the night before. We had cried while my drunken mother screamed at my father, trying to summon his wrath. We had unplugged the phone and hidden it so she couldn't call the cops in her drunken state. The last thing we needed were police officers who would take us away.

While all this was replaying in my mind, the words on the whiteboard in class might just as well have been foreign syllabics. I couldn't stop thinking about the scenes of the previous night.

I surrendered to my coping mechanisms that only created more problems for everyone.

I started drinking even more. And then I dropped out of school. It was right near the end of the eleventh grade. The Aboriginal Education worker at the high school cried the day that I quit. A part of me felt remorse, but the larger part of me didn't have the capacity to care anymore.

I hopped around from job to job, only being able to hold one for a few months before I was too drunk or hungover to make it in. I'd be fired.

I worked at a pool hall, hired by the little Italian man who befriended my father. He had kicked me out once before for drinking coolers with my friends. That night had ended with me in the drunk tank and the next day had begun with a bottle of Bacardi 151. Little Italy guy still gave me a job a few weeks later. It spoke to how much he liked my father, not to my ability to follow rules or present well.

My second job was wheeling a coffee cart around at the bingo hall. I had never seen my father's parents so many times in my life. They came to Fort St. John from Dawson for bingo all the time, yet never once did they stop by my parents' home to see us. I worked hard for those old people in the bingo hall. I made sure they had everything that they needed while they dabbed down a B-12 or an O-67. But old people in bingo halls are stingy. They don't leave tips and are extremely ritualistic. God forbid you knock one of their troll charms over while placing a coffee down. By the end of each night I'd be lucky if I made fifteen bucks.

I waitressed for a bit too, at a place owned by a nice Greek family. They were also friends of my father. The restaurant was attached to a hotel that was also attached to a stripper club. I would walk back into the narrow corridor that led to the kitchen and would always be crossing paths with dancers in their outfits. The two old Greek cooks would be playing cards and puffing on cigarettes while a girl in a cop costume and six-inch heels would walk by. No one batted an eyelash. I didn't mind working there. The tips were all right but sometimes the men who stumbled in to eat at the stripper bar were a lot less couth than the average patron.

But I lost that job as well, because one morning I was too drunk to show up. A few weeks later they asked me to come back to work but I wouldn't, out of embarrassment from my disrespect of missing a shift. I may have lost jobs routinely, but when I did work I worked hard. I got the hard work ethic from my father—even though I was a shit show. I did well wherever I worked. I'd been working since I was thirteen years old. The liquor always got the best of me, though.

Eventually, I hit a new level of hate for myself. I started to cut myself during drunken stupors. Then it got worse. I started to cut myself while I was sober.

Those brief moments of the sharp blade dragging across skin provided me with a relief from the hate that I felt for myself. It was as if the moment the skin opened up, it became a vent that poured out all of my fucked-up whirling emotions. In random places when I couldn't do this I would press my wrists down hard upon the edges of countertops and tables. Pain was the only reminder that I could feel, because I was dead inside.

One time I cut my upper thighs too deep and the cuts left big red reminders behind. I had damaged layers of skin and worried I would hit an artery one day. That would be the end of me. I didn't want to die at that time—that's not what cutting was about. I was doing it so I could put up with living.

A month after that, I took off for Edmonton again. No one at home knew that I'd been cutting. The first to find out was a random guy I met in that city.

I'd been hanging out with two friends who came with me and we decided to go to a punk rock concert. It was being held at a skate park. The Wednesday Night Heroes was a local band on stage. It was my first punk show and my body became a chaotic guitar riff as I slammed into other bodies in the mosh pit. I got punched in the arm. I got elbowed in my side. I felt alive.

After the show we stayed behind to drink beers with a few of the skateboarders.

"Helen, try to go down that ramp!" my friend squealed.

"Fuck that," I said, looking up at the ramp top that was over twice my height.

"Just doooo it!" Now both of my girls were urging me.

"Fuck it!" I said as I motioned for the dark-haired dude's skateboard.

"Put this on your head," he said as he placed his helmet on me.

I drunkenly walked my way up the steps to the top of the ramp and stood there thinking about the absolute lack of ability I had to stay on a skateboard.

"Do it!" they cheered.

I was almost ready to ride when a taller, older guy with lots of tattoos came to my side.

"You don't even have the helmet buckled," he scolded me as he clicked it together under my chin.

"You're not going down riding it. You're going to get hurt. Sit on your butt and slide down," Tall tattoo guy ordered.

I listened—knowing full well he saved my ass from getting busted up.

We drank another beer before deciding to pile into a beat-up three-seater Toyota pickup truck. It was owned by Tall tattoo guy.

"How old are you?" Tall tattoo guy wanted to know.

"Seventeen. And you?"

"Twenty-seven," he said.

We stared at each other for a moment trying to decipher the other's reaction. When we both realized that neither of us cared about bad romance, we both shrugged our shoulders.

On the ride over to his place he put his hand on my thigh. I reciprocated and placed mine on his. Later that night, after we had had sex, we showered together. It was while we were standing under a warm stream of water that he looked down and pointed at the large red scars on my legs.

"What are those from?" he asked me softly.

I closed my eyes and bowed my head as the water poured over my face. I couldn't answer him. I was too ashamed and didn't know how to articulate a lifetime of issues. But he wasn't upset by seeing the scarring. He pulled my chin up and looked me in the eyes with a softness I didn't know how to return. And then he held me. He held me in the shower, the water trickling off of our bodies, my tears mixing in with the water.

By then I had already had sex with dozens of men, but that was the first time someone I slept with had really witnessed my pain and attempted to make me feel human again.

At that time, sex and whatever soft moments came with it were still a possibility for me. It was before the incident. Before everything was taken from me.

Yes, he was far too old for me and it was highly inappropriate, but I stopped cutting after that. Yet my drinking picked up and persevered.

At times I longed for the safety of a treatment centre because it was the only place that could protect me from myself. When I was there I knew what was going to happen day in and day out. Any given moment was predictable. Out there in the real world, nothing could be foretold, and I couldn't even trust myself to keep me safe. I think this is what they call an institutionalized mindset. Yearning to be free from your own freedom.

I felt isolated and lonely and began to drink by myself again. I tried hard to hide the amount I was drinking from my family and friends. I didn't want any of my friends to know how bad it was getting for fear that they would stop drinking with me. Everything needed to remain a secret—although it was never a secret that I was an alcoholic in the first place. I started to buy mickeys of vodka and stash them around the house for when I needed a drink. I had beer bottles mixed in with clothes and stowed away just in case I needed a quick fix to ward off the shaking hands and nightmares.

The nightmares were the worst part of withdrawing for me. They scared me shitless. One time I saw an old Indian lady sitting on our living room floor. I must have been hallucinating because I would look when I was fully awake and she wasn't there. So I would pass out again. In those moments, she would reappear. I think they call this "going snakey," where your withdrawals induce hallucinations, but it always felt like I was just aware of harmful things around me.

MOM HAD BEEN sober for two years by the time I was nineteen. I was a perpetually liquored-up wilding. She showed no leniency toward me and my alcoholism. I became the hider of booze like she once was. I stashed my liquor in the same places that she had.

Drunken family irony points: 2.

I was drowning myself. I would joke around about not being able to feel and about how I had dug my heart out with a rusted spoon years before. But it was no joke. Under it all I wanted nothing more than to be free and to be able to feel. The darkness told me I would never make it. It told me to give up on the illusion of freedom. My addiction held an actual presence of darkness. A shadow that lurked in the periphery of my sober moments. Waiting. Insatiable.

I had no hope in the world until the day my son came along.

And then I lost that too.

five

THEY SAY THAT WHEN YOU DIE A LIFETIME OF MEMORY flashes before your eyes. I wasn't dead but that is what happened to me in that Edmonton hotel room. Everything I was trying to erase bubbled up with each drank I poured. The last step was to erase myself completely.

There was a knock on the door and Michael got up to answer it.

"Beers," Jimmy groaned from his bed. "Need more beers."

I reached for my purse but when the door opened I heard Alex on the other side of it.

"Uh, hey, man," his deep voice said, unsure if he had the right hotel room. "Is Helen here?"

"Who are you?" Michael questioned him.

I hadn't told them Alex was coming. I jumped up off the seat and walked to the door and opened it wide.

"Aleeexxxx!" I shrieked as I threw my arms around him.

"Hey, what's up?" he said, wrapping me in his arms.

"Let me grab my stuff and we can go downstairs for a drink."

"Drink?" he said, confused. "Since when do you drink?"

The boys started laughing hard at his confusion. "Are you fucking kidding me?" Jimmy howled. "This broad will drink you under the goddamn table!"

"Shut the fuck up, Jimmy," I said as I tossed a pillow at him.

Jimmy was still laughing. "Easy now, I'm just spittin' facts here!"

"I'll be back, guys," I said as I grabbed Alex by the hand and led him out.

"Who are those guys?" Alex questioned me.

"Just some guys from home."

"You know them, though?"

"Yeah, since I was young."

"How in the hell did you end up here with them, Helen?"

"Things . . . ," I said as the elevator doors closed, "things are fucked up right now, Alex."

"What do you mean?"

"I'm fucking out of it . . . ," I said in a low voice. "I'm done for."

"Jesus, Helen, I didn't even know you started drinking. Things must be fucked up for you right now if you're hitting the bottle this hard."

"I fucked things up. I did that."

"Did what? I don't know what you mean."

"Just . . . I don't want to get into it right now," I replied. "I can't."

The doors opened and I led Alex to the small hotel bar. We ordered some drinks. Alex stared at me like I was one of those hologram pictures you gawk at until you go cross-eyed. Maybe he was trying to see the hidden picture?

"What the fuck, Alex? What are you lookin' at?" I said as I pushed his shoulder playfully, trying to mask my level of unease.

"I'm sorry, but it's just bizarre seeing you like this," he said. He stared down into his drink before taking a big gulp.

"This is it," I said. This was it. Me drinking—this is all there would ever be, I thought.

"When you going home?"

"I'm not."

"What do you mean you're not?"

"Exactly what I said," I said, staring at the table.

Alex didn't respond. I knew he was waiting for me to tell him more and stop with my cryptic bullshit.

"Things have been really bad, I keep fucking up. I can't stay sober for the goddamned life of me, Alex," I spat out. Teeth gritted, jaw clenched, and eyes blinking back the tears. "I . . . I can't go home anymore. I fucked everything up and I'm just going to keep going wherever. I don't know where, but I'm just going to go," I said.

"Helen," Alex said softly, "I don't really think running away is the answer. Now, I knew you when you were sober and you seemed to be able to do that real well. Shit, a whole lot better than me! I don't know when you slept last, but you look like you could use some of that too. Maybe you just need to rest and get a clear mind."

"I'm not asking you for advice. This is what I'm doing and I don't want to talk about it anymore," I said coldly.

"All right, all right. Easy now, girl, we can talk about something else. Here—cheers me to the first time of us ever drinking together. This is a bloody trip."

Our glasses clinked and I downed my drink.

"Now about those guys you're with . . ."

Alex didn't trust me with them and insisted that I stay with him so he could watch over me. I knew the men I was with were harmless and wanted to take care of me. But they did represent my closest ties to home, and I needed to cut even the last of the cords.

Alex stood brooding in the hotel room doorway as I gathered my things. The boys stared at him with daggers shooting from their eyes.

"Are you sure you're going to be okay?" Michael asked.

"Don't worry about me, Michael. I'll figure shit out," I said. But I knew that I was lying to him and to myself.

"Be safe . . . ." Michael's big brown eyes stared at me, pleading.

I looked at him and shrugged my shoulders with a half-nod of my head as if to say that I could only try my best.

"Here's one hundred for some of the room cost," I said as I placed money on the table.

"All right," Jimmy said from the bed.

I hugged both of them while Alex picked up my bags, and I walked out. I was definitely not going home now.

I knew that Alex meant well, but I think he purposefully miscalculated where I would be more vulnerable. I was no longer the untouchable woman with my boundaries and preferred-mate check boxes to be ticked. We went to his place and he mixed us a drink before we went upstairs to his room. The house was full of the noise and presence of roommates, who were also drinking. I didn't want to be around other people. My anxiety came more often now that I was running longer with no sleep.

"I need fucking cocaine," I said angrily as I plopped down on Alex's mattress.

"You do cocaine now too?" he asked with a laugh of disbelief.

"There's a lot you don't know about me," I said, letting out a sigh.

"I have some."

"You have some what?"

"Coke."

"Well, what the fuck are you waiting for? Bust it out."

"No."

"No?" I repeated.

"No," he said again firmly.

"Are you fucking kidding me right now?" I said in annoyance.

"No, Helen, I'm not," he replied. "I have never in my life seen you like this, and I am not about to give you fucking blow. Jesus, I haven't even seen you drink before."

"Listen, Alex," I said in a sharp tone, "it's not like I'm trying coke for the first fucking time here. I have been doing a lot. Obscene fucking amounts. So get off the high road and cut that shit up because now that I know you have it, I will not fucking drop it. Maybe you should have left me with those other guys. At least I could do whatever the fuck I wanted."

Silence.

Alex took a deep breath and reached into his dresser. The plastic-bagged messiah. The white girl. Co-fucking-caine. My body un-tensed. We drank, we did more cocaine, and we drank. Finally it came to that moment, the moment that had been coming since I had texted him. Alex kissed me.

"I always wanted to do that," he said.

"I know," I whispered and kissed him back. I had never wanted to kiss him.

It progressed quickly and before I knew it he was tugging on the button of my jeans. I started to panic.

"No . . ." I said and pushed his hand away.

"Okay," he whispered and kissed me softly.

He tried again.

"I can't," I told him, and my heart started to beat out of my chest. My head started to swirl. I pushed him off of me and sat upright. I started to cry. The floodgates finally opened and I couldn't hold them back anymore.

"Whoa, I'm sorry, Helen," Alex said. "What's wrong? Was it me? I'm sorry."

"They fucking cut me," I choked out between my sobs. "They . . . fucking . . . cut . . . me."

"What do you mean, Helen?" Alex asked, a hint of anger flashing in his voice. "Who cut you? What happened?"

I lay on my side and tried to cry as quietly as I could.

I hadn't told anyone about that night.

I DON'T REMEMBER it happening. It was my twenty-fourth birthday and I wanted to dance that night to loud music in pretty shoes. I put on the green vest that a freckled friend had given me the month before when I was visiting Toronto. "The world is yours, Helen, you just have to go for it," she'd said to me as we walked under the city lights. That night was going to be *my* night. I walked into the bar on a mission and I received free birthday drinks from men. I drank with a sailor's zeal to catch up.

My last memory before morning was being in an over-crowded apartment just a few blocks from home and the bed I should have been sleeping in.

The men outnumbered the women five to one. This was not abnormal for Fort St. John, where there are so many male transient workers. It is raining men in oil and gas territory, and no one is crying out *hallelujah*. But no one is saying *enough*, either. I thought nothing of it until the morning.

Two women.

Ten men.

No memory.

I knew—I felt—I sensed—something was deeply wrong.

Something very bad had happened in that overcrowded place. I found the courage to ask the girl who had accompanied me, "What happened?" My voice cracked like the earth splitting from beneath me.

The girl was an introduction away from being a stranger. She stared at the floor nervously before she all but vomited the words out of her mouth. She told me that she yelled at them when she found me on the floor. Curse words crashed into each other. They had me there on the floor. Three of them. She spoke so rapidly that I couldn't follow her as she jumped through the story.

"Those fucking assholes," she said shaking her head. "That's when we fucking left."

I asked her again, much quieter this time, "What happened?"

I watched her eyes cloud over and the truth become hidden behind them. "I . . . I can't remember," she said as she shifted her gaze downward. I asked again. She did not offer up any more truth and left me with only more questions.

Later that morning, I stood in the shower. A river of red ran out of me. My hands moved slowly—I was scared to discover the damage. I was cut badly. My clitoris wept. My fingers ran over the swollen bulb of flesh that seemed to be barely hanging on. I winced at the pain. I drew my hand back and stared at the blood on my fingers in shock. I began to disconnect from my body and reality. Whose blood was this? Whose blood did I have on my hands?

I sat in the shower, arms folded over knees and I cried as the blood disappeared down the drain. I couldn't remember what had happened, but my body bled red tears for days after.

My body was not my own.

I was no longer my own.

I had never been my own.

AFTER THAT, I slept with my hands over my ovaries like my fingerprints could speak memory to the woman who was dying inside of me. I wondered if I could ever have children again. I prayed that some men's violent and sick sexual leanings hadn't stolen my future children's cries and the words I would say to soothe them.

Violence reverberates and lives long after the semen is washed away. After the bruises fade and the bleeding stops, the monster left behind eats up the light like no beast I've ever known. The body is capable of absorbing a multitude of violent acts and continuing to live, but it is the spirit that breaks under the weight of it.

That's what happened to me. A part of me died that day and I silenced myself. I believed that what had happened was my fault and that I'd had some part in instigating such a violent act.

In fact, every rape that had happened to me hung over my head like a crown of thorns. I told myself in the still moments that I must have done something to allow that. There is something wrong with me and I brought all this upon myself. When the anxiety threatened to push me to an emotional place I was sure I wouldn't come out of I would tell myself, *It will be like the other times, Helen. You have been raped before and you survived. Just shut up and move forward. Shut up. Move forward.*

Within a few days, my body stopped bleeding, but shame and self-hatred poured down on me. Those feelings were always there, a scratch beneath the surface at any given time. The years of sexual abuse. The rapes. The decade of self-punishment. What happened that night had only opened the floodgates.

The unknown night and discovery of violence was traumatizing and caused me nightmares. Even though I couldn't remember. Even though I blacked out. No space felt safe for me, not even the dream world.

After this, I pledged to myself I would never black out. My saviour and solution to this nuisance of blacking out came in the form of a white powder. I would no longer drink without coke to keep me in check. Then it became more and more about the cocaine and I found myself returning home after days spent bingeing, not realizing just how much time had passed.

How many times had my son asked for me?

I was disappearing regularly and now my child was suffering from my neglect. I did that. Me. I neglected him while trying to erase wounds from my mind and body.

I thank Creator for my mom during this time—and I thank Creator that she'd found sobriety. It was my mom who was there for Mathias. She was his source of dependability when I could not be.

I knew that in the hardness of my hangovers and his need for my attention, I couldn't give him what he needed. So I would do the minimum. I did my best to cope with the few tools I could find. I would get him to sit in bed with me and watch movies while we ate popsicles. He would love me, with all of his unease, and I needed him to be present so that I could feel human. Mathias made me feel human. Like I was worthy. I sponged off of his light because I only knew darkness.

Sometimes if I thought too long and hard on it I could hear his lonely footsteps running to the room to check if his mother had made it home the night before. The footsteps of neglect. It is incredibly hard to know that the only person I never wanted to disappoint in life was not safe from my flawed being.

This love, you would think, could save me. I thought that the love for my child would be a raft of sorts—to pull me from the raging waters of addiction. But my addicted mind and crippled spirit used the same love to shame me. And I found myself drowning. When I lay in bed at night my sober awareness amplified everything I couldn't put words to. The darkness always flooded in. The voices in my head roared.

You will never have children again.
You are a fuck-up.
No one will ever love you now.
You will die old and alone.
You will never have children again.
You are a fuck-up.
No one will ever love you now.

THIS WAS THE story I had been holding on to.

"They cut me" is all I could manage to tell Alex.

I couldn't turn around to face him, not when I was blubbering like a lunatic in his bed. I was crying against my will and my internal voice was saying things like *How pathetic, Helen. Such a fuckin' baby.*

"Do you want to talk about it more?" Alex asked me.

I shook my head. He lay down beside me, placing his hand on my shoulder. His kindness and his presence comforted me. Finally, I drifted off to sleep.

It didn't last long. I woke up later—contracting and expanding. Alex had left my side during slumber. He appeared again bearing food and tried to get me back to sleep. This is where my story begins. This is where the story of who I really am under the layers of addiction surfaces and where the story of how I reclaimed *Dishinit Sakeh* begins. I was sweat-soaked and starfishing in bed. Alex's body failed to constrain me as I twisted around. He left me alone again to face my beasts in solitude.

My hands shook. My body vibrated. I reached over the edge of the bed and started shifting through discarded heaps of clothing to find my phone.

My friend Ellie in Ontario had put a call out for people to bombard me with love and light-filled messages because I needed them. She had seen the me that existed under all of the pain I hid myself under. I had texts, inbox messages, and wall posts from people I had crossed paths with over the years across the country. I clutched my phone, shaking in the fetal position, and read messages like "You are a strong and beautiful warrior, and are able to conquer anything," and "We love you so much and life would not be good without you."

One text was from a little boy who was eleven years old, with whom I had connected the summer before. I was doing a community placement and his family opened their home to me while I did my work. When I brought my son to their community, the boys played together and I became close with his family. Sadly, later that same year, winter hit and the hard times followed. The boy's father lost a long battle with addiction and committed suicide. I remembered the pain of his loss and how sad I was for him and his family. My heart ached for them.

That same young boy was one of those who texted me—in my hour of need.

Helen where r u

Please helen b ok

There is so much loss in our communities, so much loss suffered by our people and children. I couldn't add to that loss. We have become far too accustomed to loss. I couldn't leave that gaping hole, especially for my son.

My son.

My son.

I have a son and his name is Mathias.

I dropped the phone on the bed.

My body wrenched. I moaned and expanded in a quick and violent movement.

I wanted to die, but more of me wanted to live. I reached back across the bed for my phone, my hands shook. Ellie's light had spread and I dialled the number home.

"Is that you, my girl?" my mom's voice said softly.

"Yes, Mama . . . it's me," I whispered.

"My girl," my mom said cautiously, "can you come home now?"

"Mama," I cried, "aren't you better off without me?"

I burst into tears, almost choking in the process.

"No, no, no," my mom said, "we need you and we love you."

I cried even harder.

"Where are you, my girl?"

"Edmonton."

"Okay, well, we need to get you home. Who are you with? Are you safe?"

"I'm . . . I'm okay. I'm good. I'm just . . . I'm sick. But I'm okay."

"I'm going to see who can pick you up, okay? Are you still drinking?"

"No . . ."

I moaned as I contracted.

"Are you sure you're okay? Maybe you need to go to the hospital."

"Mmmmm . . ."

"My girl, it's serious. Sometimes you have to go do those things with people to watch you," she urged me.

"No," I replied, "I can't . . . I'll . . . I'll be okay."

"Okay, but if it gets worse, promise me you'll go in?"

"Mom, I should've . . ."

"Should've what, Helen?"

"Should've gone to treatment, Mom. I was so scared. I should have gone."

"It's okay, my girl. We will get you into one when we get back but let's just get you home for now. I'm going to call and see if Kat can pick you up."

"Kat?"

"Kat, your auntie's friend, who lives in Fort Saskatchewan. Then we will get you home."

"Mmmm . . ."

"Okay I'm going to hang up now and then I'll call back."

"Mmmm . . ."

"Helen, please answer when I call back . . . please," she said, her voice plagued with fear and sadness.

"I will, Mama . . ." I promised.

Within an hour, Kat pulled into the parking lot of Alex's house and he walked me outside. I wanted to recede into a dark hole and never emerge.

"I'm glad you're going home, Helen. It's the right thing," Alex said as he hugged me goodbye.

I managed a weak smile.

Kat got out of her vehicle and walked toward me, a serious but soft look on her face. She hugged me and nodded wearily toward Alex. Kat had been my auntie's friend since they were teenagers. She was a tall, blonde, no-bullshit kind of woman who did hard jobs men could do but did them even better.

"C'mon girl," she said, "let's get you to my place."

I sat in the vehicle feeling like an alien specimen.

She must be able to see how fucked up I am, I thought. The anxiety crept in quickly. It was daytime, and I was blatantly disgusting.

"So what's going on?" she asked me nonchalantly.

"I'm . . . just fucked up."

"Everybody fucks up, girl. Everyone," she said. "You do so much, Helen. You may not know this but I talk about you to people I know. I told my boyfriend about how you went to Switzerland and spoke at the United Nations. We all fuck up. You'll be okay."

"How do you know?" I whispered as I stared out the window.

"You've been through so much already and look how much you've done. Shit, you even built schools in Nicaragua! Most people don't do that kind of stuff in their entire life, Helen. I know you'll pull through," Kat answered with conviction in her voice.

What she said helped me a bit. It forced me to remember. The cobblestone streets and smiling children of Nicaragua and the swans of Lake Geneva. It seemed like they had never been a part of my reality as I sat withdrawing in the passenger seat of Kat's vehicle. They were memories that no longer belonged to me.

And yet, they were mine. My accomplishments. I have done good in this world.

I am not all darkness.

Kat reminded me.

six

THAT TRIP ABROAD WAS A FEW YEARS BEFORE, WHEN I turned twenty-one. That's when a friend came to me with an invitation I couldn't refuse. I held unrealized dreams of travel inside of me. The task? To build a school in Nicaragua.

At the time, I felt like things were coming together. I was going to school full time again. I was on the student council. Most importantly, I was trying to be the best parent I could to my chubby, handsome son.

The Nicaragua trip was being organized by the Indigenous Youth Empowering Students (IYES) program. It was through an organization called Schoolbox. I knew that if I was to go, I would have to fundraise every single cent. And I would have to be creative. As a young single mother and student, I didn't even have extra cash to buy another bus pass if I lost mine.

My friend Kyla and I signed up together. We got accepted and did our best to come up with ideas on how to raise money. We also had to plan out a cultural presentation. We were going to talk about our Indigenous cultures here in Canada. I didn't really know a lot about who I was. It was one of the first times in my life that I started to ask questions about the people to which I belong.

The Dane Zaa and the Cree.

I went to my asu for help.

She told me stories, like she used to do when I was little. Stories like how the crow became black. I paid more attention this time. She taught me how to introduce myself in my Dane Zaa language. I helped out at the local powwow and learned about smudging and medicines.

I started to feel proud about who I am, and it was a new feeling that I embraced wholeheartedly. At the same time, I was taking an Introduction to First Nations Studies course. Things we discussed in that course upset me. It's where I began to learn about all of the oppressive policies and genocidal madness that Native people have faced in Canadian history. Sometimes I would get so angry that I'd throw my book across the room. Other times, I'd be taken over by grief and cry over my textbooks. I was in a state of active reclamation and recovery.

I became more focused on finding out who I am.

So, our planning for our trip began with great enthusiasm but apparently not such great ideas. Our first great fundraising concept was to throw a punk rock concert.

We dubbed it Punk Rock for Pura Vida. I wrote proposals modelled from a book someone had lent me. One idea was to find free giveaway items and approach hotels to see if they would donate a free overnight stay. We wrote messages to punk rock bands in the region and soon enough we had five bands respond. We had some organization's free gas so that our punk rock performers would be able to make the trip.

The plan was paved with good intentions but not well executed. It turns out there is no money in punk rock. Surprise! The bands played. We danced. We slammed into audience members. We did our spiel on stage. We were still broke. One of the musicians who made the trip even donated one hundred dollars to us out of pity.

"We're not going now." Kyla was hitting faith rock bottom a few days later as we sat in a quiet stairwell downtown.

"Don't talk like that," I said. "Remember what I told you I heard that woman say?"

"I know, I know," Kyla said.

"If what you're doing is right, and if what you're doing is good, then what you need will find you."

"But Helen, we only have two weeks left to plan this trip and we still need fourteen hundred dollars in order to go!" Kyla whined.

"I don't care. It's happening. We're going to Nicaragua," I stated firmly.

It was at this very moment that fate smiled upon us. I noticed a vehicle pass by and, for some reason, it caught my attention. On the back of that car was a sticker for a local muffler shop.

"There," I announced to Kyla and I pointed at the sticker.

"What?" Kyla asked.

"We are going to that muffler shop."

"You're fucking kidding me, right? A muffler shop? Why would anyone there care about building a school in Nicaragua?"

"Shut it down, Kyla. Let's go," I said as I stood up and walked toward where the car had come to a stop.

"Okay, but you're asking," she said uneasily.

We walked into that muffler shop carrying the proposal papers that explained our efforts. Truth be told, I didn't know what I was doing and thought it was also crazy as hell to be walking into a place like that and asking for a donation. But I was determined. I shook off the feeling and approached the front desk. We were greeted by a big man who had several tattoos.

"Hi, ummm, is the owner in?" I asked shyly.

"That would be me," he said without meeting my eyes.

I explained our fundraising efforts and how much we had earned, or had not earned, and what we wanted to do. I pushed the papers I was carrying across the countertop. Kyla couldn't even look at me. I could tell she was embarrassed to be standing there.

The man at the muffler shop showed no emotion. He glanced at the paper. Then he asked a pointed question: "So, what do you need?"

"Donations," I said.

He reached down into the cash drawer and pulled out several bills. He placed them in front of me. "Here's three hundred. Is that good?" he asked.

"Wow!" I said in disbelief. "Yeah, that helps so much!"

He smiled for the first time.

"Thank you!" I squealed.

"Yeah, no problem," he said casually.

I grabbed the cash and walked out with a stunned Kyla at my side.

"I told you," I said as we headed for our vehicle.

"A bloody muffler shop," Kyla said, shaking her head. "Who'd have guessed?" Her doubts were erased. Four days after that, we had enough money to go to Nicaragua.

But even then, it wasn't smooth sailing.

To get to Managua, we had to fly from Calgary. That meant catching a bus.

What is it people say about the road to hell?

We missed the bus on a stopover in another city. Kyla wanted to buy a watch to keep track of time. As we walked back to the bus station we watched a Greyhound bus pull out of the station.

"Oh my God! Is that our bus?!" Kyla exclaimed.

"Settle down. Our bus doesn't leave for another fifteen minutes," I said coolly.

We walked into the station to find empty gleaming linoleum floors and seats that weren't filled with bodies. It was, in fact, our bus. We had to get on that bus. It required some quick thinking and meant we'd have to be creative and resourceful one more time.

We flagged down a cab. And like some scene in a movie, we asked the driver to speed ahead.

"Dude . . . how do we pull over a bus?" I laughed as we barrelled down the road.

With the meter running and a lack of ideas on how to successfully pull over a bus, we found ourselves on the side of the road outside of town with our thumbs out in the hot summer heat.

"This is a sign, Helen—we should go home," Kyla said as a car whizzed past us.

"Fuck that," I said. "Nothing can stop us."

Kyla dragged her feet as we marched forward. I could only smile and laugh at what was quickly becoming a calamity. These kinds of challenges made me feel alive.

It didn't take long before we got picked up. The driver was a young man, probably in his thirties. He liked to do impressions of movie characters, and apparently he liked the feeling of the pedal under his heavy foot. We sailed down the highway at 160 kilometres an hour while he transformed into Jim Carrey and Christopher Walken.

I remembered that the bus had a stopover in Edmonton. I told our new driver that we would need to get dropped off at the bus depot there to get our onboard bags. He drove so fast that we beat the bus to the Edmonton depot by two whole hours. We thanked the brown-haired Danny DeVito–talking man named Ian.

We said goodbye. But in less than twenty minutes I received a text from an unfamiliar number.

Have a good trip.

Who is this? I texted back.

It's Ian.

Ian? The guy who just dropped us off?

Yes :)

Ian . . . how did you get my number?

I have a device in my car that picks up and stores numbers.

Oh . . .

Just kidding!! I bet you thought that was creepy. When you went and used the bathroom I texted myself from your phone.

Ian.

Yes?

That's creepy too.

When the bus finally pulled up to the platform, we stood at the front like well-versed road warriors waiting to get our luggage. Can't stop us! Won't stop us! It was the look our stoic Indigenous faces conveyed.

Kyla was paranoid after that. As our big suitcases came off that bus, she asked if we needed to grab them. I assured her there were baggage handlers who did that. But she wasn't satisfied with my answer and asked one of the workers. The worker repeated what I'd just said and told her that he would handle the baggage transfers.

When we finally arrived in Calgary it was midnight. Our luggage had not made the trip. It was probably still sitting on that Edmonton platform. So much for the assurances of that baggage guy.

Kyla was so upset that for a while she couldn't even speak. We walked around Calgary with our small backpacks. Then it started to rain.

"I'm definitely not going now! Fuck fuck fuuuuuck!" Kyla screamed in frustration.

"It's just clothes," I said.

I was in a state of disbelief that was mixed with a bit of amusement. But the novelty of our situation was slowly wearing off. We made a telephone call to the founder of the organization that was hosting the trip. He told us to come anyway, offering encouragement: "Whenever you are close to a breakthrough, that's when obstacles are placed on your path." We listened to his sage advice while hiding from the rain under the awning of a shop.

WE MADE IT to Nicaragua.

Stepping off the plane was like opening the door to a sauna. The humid heat engulfed our northern-acclimatized bodies as we walked down the ramp and into a strange new world. The security guards at the Managua airport looked at us weird when we passed through customs with no baggage for them to check.

"We made it," I smiled at Kyla. We walked toward the arrival area and a sea of waiting people, looking for the ones there to greet us.

My eyes hungrily ate up every sight as we drove from the airport to where we would stay for the night. Even the architecture was foreign, with small concrete-block buildings that had brightly coloured sheet metal roofs. From what I could tell, the shops doubled as homes. People were everywhere. The streets were alive. Music filled my ears. The sounds of people yelling and talking loudly in Spanish spilled into the vehicle. There was a steady pulse of pedestrians in the roadway, on the sidewalk, and in the meridians between lanes. Excitement and energy poured out from every direction. Children walked around in flip-flops or barefooted. Mamas carried large weaved trays on their hips. Those platters were laden with fresh sliced fruit and unidentifiable cooked goods, which they offered for sale to motorists stopped at a red light. Little girls and boys held smaller trays and did the same or held plastic baggies full of juice or water to sell to thirsty travellers. The smell of fried food filled our vehicle. I saw young boys walking on the roadside with a giant dead lizard hanging from a wooden pole that they carried over their shoulders. The lizard was dinner. Sometimes, an ox and cart would be side by side with a fancy luxury car at a stoplight. The fancier shopping complexes were few and far between. But when I did spot one, it was protected by large brick walls around the entryway and small turrets with guards holding big guns.

I found this disparity of wealth disturbing.

The next day we departed to Leon, and I watched a bustling, colourful world from the back-seat window. When we pulled up to the school grounds where we would be building four new classrooms, a line of children stood waving balloons above their heads. I almost wept as I exited the vehicle and was greeted in Spanish by dozens of chattering kids. I was right where I was supposed to be, doing the work I was supposed to do.

I spent some mornings with the women of the village cooking rice, beans, and plantains in the church next door. I played with the kids with a football we'd brought from home—that is, when they were able to have a break. A lot of the older children volunteered to work alongside the men, hauling cinder blocks. Their young faces showed more dedication than I've witnessed in grown men working back home.

Everyone was excited about the new school.

We mixed cement by shovel. We cut rebar under the blazing sun. Little girls would come up and give us notes written in Spanish with drawings sketched out inside them. It was a life-changing experience that allowed me to realize how grateful I was for this education. I was a young single Indigenous mother but I had never known poverty like this. I never had to put my son to bed knowing he was still hungry. Yet despite the poverty, I saw love, strength, and hope in the people I met.

It puzzled me one morning as I watched a man plunk hard beans into a red plastic pail. We were on our way to the work site.

"What's he doing?" I asked the woman who was our group leader.

She spoke to the man in Spanish and he explained. "He is measuring the food for his family for the day," she said as we walked away.

My heart ached. I felt bad for walking away without being able to offer a solution. My heart ached for the hard beans in that red plastic pail. My guess was that not every mouth would be fed.

Also on that first day, I remember seeing a young man stop his bicycle near the entrance to our job site. He stared at us. He was around my age and had a few tattoos on his arm and one on his face. He looked on with curiosity as we went inside the school. On our third day there, he showed up to volunteer and help build the classrooms. I would catch him staring at my tattoos in between cutting rebar for the pillars.

During one of my breaks, I walked across an empty lot. Kids played soccer there sometimes. Moments later, I noticed our new volunteer trailing behind me.

"*Hola*," I said.

"*Hola*," he said, nodding at me.

"*Como se llama*?" I asked.

"*Alberto, y tú*?"

Utilizing what little Spanish language I knew, I told him that I had nothing to offer in conversation. "Helen. *Yo hablo muy poquito Español*," I said. "Umm . . . *cuantos años tienes* [how old are you]?"

"*Veintidós* [twenty-two]," he replied.

I moved to the next one of the four questions I knew how to ask. "Umm . . . *tienes hermanos . . . hermanas* [do you have brothers/sisters]?"

"*Sí, siete hermanos* [yes, seven brothers]," Alberto answered as he kicked up dust.

"Ahh, *bueno* [good]," I said.

"No," he answered.

"*Por que* [why]?" I asked, trying to make sense of his comment.

"*Siete hermanos, muerte*," he said.

"*Muerte*?" I asked.

"*Sí*," he said as he bent over to draw a cross in the sand and then pointed at the blue sky above us. "*Muerte*."

Dead.

Seven brothers.

I nodded my head as he bowed his slightly. Slowly, Alberto walked back toward the school grounds. The cross in the sand lay at my feet. It reminded me again of the fragility of life.

That image is always with me. Even here, in Kat's vehicle under this blue Albertan sky, I can see Alberto's brown face staring upwards trying to catch a glimpse of the afterlife. Life is so impermanent.

And yet, even through that reality and that sadness, there was such beauty in what the IYES program was attempting to do. We made a real difference in the lives of many, and at the same time, our lives were altered forever by the people we met in Nicaragua. I was proud in those moments— proud of what we accomplished, but also proud of who I was becoming. That is what drew me back to that country. Two years later in 2011, a group of us returned a second time to expand on the project. This time, we built a school in a small mining town called Bella Vista, where the kids carried their chairs to school and the teacher hitchhiked both ways.

During this second trip, I was able to visit the school that we had helped build on my first trip. I took pictures of the four new classrooms. They were filled with desks and with smiling, curious brown faces. It brought such warmth to my heart.

Before long, I was on my way back to Canada. On the last stretch of my flight I settled into my seat next to a man who looked familiar, but I couldn't quite place him.

"So is Vancouver home or is Fort St. John?" I asked.

"Fort St. John is. I was just down here getting some new ink for my sleeve," he answered, lifting up his arm.

"Oh, cool. I have a few tattoos myself. Are you going to get more?"

"Yeah, I want both arms done so I'm always making trips down to see the artist here. He does amazing work."

It was then that I recognized the man.

"Do you by chance work at a muffler shop?" I asked.

"Yeah, I own one in town," he said.

I smiled and explained my questioning. "Two years ago you gave me money to build a school. I just went down to Nicaragua to build another school and I got to visit the finished classrooms from the first time. I got pictures! Do you want to see the school you helped build?" I asked excitedly.

"What? That's crazy! I remember that. Yeah, let's see them," he exclaimed.

I was stunned at life. It further solidified my belief that life is about living for others and that the universe/Creator/ God was watching over me.

So many positive thoughts to remember while Kat continued to drive and I stared out at the passing landscape. Kat was right. I have done good things. Those moments felt so far away and fleeting, but they were closer to my grasp now. I was returning home to the person I love most in this world.

His name is Mathias.

"So what was Switzerland like?" Kat asked as she continued to navigate the highway lanes.

"It was beautiful. Beautiful and cold," I replied. My body shook not from memory but from the continued withdrawal.

A few months before the brutal assault on me, I was distracted with trying to create change and still had a bit of a hold on life. ·

I had applied to be part of a different trip overseas. As an Indigenous Youth Ambassador I would be going to the United Nations in Geneva, Switzerland. We were to present testimony about the inequalities facing Indigenous children and youth in the areas of education, child welfare, and health care. Canada has been failing and continues to fail Indigenous people.

I made it to the second stage of participant selection and had to do a three-person-panel phone interview. I prayed for both strength and confidence, lighting some sage to cleanse my thoughts. I smudged myself, offering gratitude that I had made it this far in the process. I asked Spirit to guide me to know the right words to speak. I prayed that the right people were sent to Switzerland. People who could carry voice. And in case it wasn't me, I prayed for the people who would be chosen to go.

For days after the interview, I sat and visualized a positive outcome. I'd be in the living room with my eyes closed, imagining Switzerland. I imagined the sounds, the sights, and the people I would meet. I imagined what it would feel like to get the call that told me I was going, and how happy I would be.

The next day I got the call. I was going to Toronto for training and then heading off to Switzerland.

There was no foreshadowing the traumatic act of violence that would take place just a few weeks after I was accepted. I had been sober for a few months before that and I don't know what led me to the bar that night. It was my birthday. I wanted to dance. I had a million reasons to go out. I deserved to celebrate. It was going to be fun this time. Alcoholics have a way of convincing themselves that "this time will be different." The times may be different but the fact that I am an alcoholic never changes.

I didn't see it coming. It broke my spirit and made me want to back out from attending this important forum.

There are bigger problems in the world, I told myself. There are bigger problems in the world, I told myself when I started to crumble under my spirit's weight. There are bigger problems in the world, I said as I lay awake at night with my hands over my ovaries. You have dealt with rape before, I whispered to myself—just hold on.

There were six of us who made the trip to Geneva. We represented a mix of urban and rural backgrounds. Each was amazing, with unique passions and experiences. One young man was fluent in the Cree language and had been raised with the knowledge of his Treaty. Another had thrived in life in spite of being in the foster care system. One girl came from Attawapiskat and talked about her friend, the late Shannen Koostachin, who had fought for the same investment in education for First Nations children in First Nations communities. Shannen had died while attending school away from her community. This girl picked up where her friend had left off in order to make changes that are necessary for First Nations children across the country. The movement is called Shannen's Dream.

We did media training for the scheduled news conferences we'd have to face once in Geneva. Facilitators taught us how to answer questions and how to make the most use of our social media accounts to build up hype and stay connected.

I met Cindy Blackstock. Let me repeat that: I met Cindy Blackstock. She is the woman behind the First Nations Child and Family Caring Society. I so admired her for launching a human rights case against the Canadian federal government. It charged that the government discriminates against First Nations with respect to unequal funding for child welfare and social services. I had, and still have, a huge social-justice crush on Cindy Blackstock. Everything that came out of her mouth was like a prepared statement, full of genuine heart and calculated thoughts.

I have a list of Indigenous female crushes whom I want to meet. Powerhouses. Trailblazers. Warriors.

We stood at the top of a high-rise in downtown Toronto just after we finished that first news conference—letting the press know why we were headed to Switzerland. I stared out the window. And even though it was bleak outside, I felt like I was on top of the world.

Two short days later we boarded for Switzerland. Alanis Obamsawin, the renowned Canadian filmmaker, had joined us. She wanted to chronicle our journey and use the clips in one of her upcoming documentaries. Alanis was an elegant woman, speaking with her rich French accent. She had an air about her that made you pull your shoulders back and hold your head up high.

On that flight, the sound of different languages floated in the air. The excitement of reaching new soil filled my spirit. I sat beside a gentleman from Togo who was on his way to defend his dissertation for his PhD. He courteously held my hand when we hit turbulence while flying over the ocean. It helped that he was handsome.

"It will be okay," he laughed as I squeezed his hand, "that wasn't even bad turbulence."

I squeezed harder.

ON OUR FIRST day in Geneva I walked for blocks in the narrow streets. The stores sold Swiss army knives and cheap souvenirs alongside high-end Rolex watches and designer clothing. I ventured into chocolatier shops that were filled with sweet aromas. I would return to those shops over the course of our stay, buying small bags of delicately hand-crafted sweets that I devoured in my tiny European-sized room. I walked down to the water and stood beside the bridge, staring at Lake Geneva's vastness. I watched the swans in the water each day. The winter air surrounded me and I took a deep breath, thinking of the days to come. I was in Switzerland and was going to the United Nations. I had imagined this moment.

Now, I was here. The time was too busy to remember what had happened to me.

On our second day, we toured one of the UN buildings and I bought trinkets for my family and a T-shirt for my son. We met with a reporter in the afternoon. That evening, I did an APTN interview via Skype with another youth ambassador and Cindy Blackstock. I was hyped on social justice. I retired to my room to go over my notes and prepare for the following day. We were meeting with members of the United Nations during a pre-session on how Canada is upholding its adhesion to the UN Convention on the Rights of the Child (UNCRC). A pre-session is where other countries come together to review each country's actions and where they are failing and succeeding in regards to various UN conventions.

All of us were jittery as we passed through two security check stations. From there, we waited in a room with tall, richly dark wooden walls and a window that overlooked Lake Geneva.

Traditionally, the organizations that were providing shadow reports (counter-reports to the federal government's report on how it is meeting the UNCRC) were allotted a few minutes to speak. There were a few organizations that had helped bring our Indigenous Youth Ambassador delegation together and they each threw in some of their time, which was limited at best. We were each allotted only thirty seconds to speak, so those thirty seconds had to matter.

We came to say that Canada is failing Indigenous peoples.

When we were finally escorted to the conference room, we were seated in front of a long wooden table with microphones available for each speaker. My hands were sweaty and shaking. The tall Ojibwe ambassador and I looked at each other and exchanged knowing, nervous smiles.

After we spoke, the committee made it clear that they weren't impressed with what we had come to say. We were essentially told that the UN is no place for personal testimonies. All of us, except for the Indigenous Youth Ambassador who worked on Shannen's Dream, had spoken from a personal point of view. We tried to tie in a quick story that linked our concerns to our specific territories. I talked about the level of gender-based violence within the territory I was from and how that placed Indigenous girls and women at risk. We have a high number of missing and murdered Indigenous women in our area, while Indigenous people make up only a small percentage of the overall population.

After we had finished, and prior to the organizations beginning to provide overviews of their reports, is when the committee said they were there to listen to facts and relevant specifics only. My face flushed and I wriggled in my seat like a scolded child. After it was over, many of the heads of other organizations approached us and apologized for the abrasive reception we had received from the committee. They said they planned to issue a letter of complaint on our behalf. Later, we received an apology.

We discussed this as a group later on. We talked about how it felt and if we thought we were really making a difference. The answer was a resounding yes. All of us came from different places across Canada, which pulled in the attention of various communities. We had all done pre-interviews locally and regionally, on radio stations and for print and online publications. It did contribute to the awareness that was being built on a national level at home: Canada has been messing up so bad that young Indigenous people had to travel to the United Nations.

Canada has been, and still is, failing the Indigenous people.

And the time for our youth to remain silent was over. We spoke—and will continue to do so. We were sent to Geneva for a reason and with purpose. At the end of the day, I decided to trust in that belief.

ON THE LAST night in Geneva, I treated myself to a meal at a high-end restaurant. I went with one of the other participants. The restaurant sat alongside the water's edge. We had seen it the day before on a walk across the bridge and longed to try its menu.

"I want to eat there!" she had exclaimed, pointing at the restaurant that had glass walls facing the lake. She was a self-proclaimed foodie and had insisted on taking pictures of every dinner plate since we had landed. We tried Indian food together and it was amazing. At another establishment, to our utter disappointment, we tried a big pot of fondue that no one at the table could eat. When she pointed out this restaurant I asked if I could join her. She made the reservation and we walked to the bougie five-star restaurant together.

The hostess seated us, and our waiter laid a cloth napkin across each of our laps. He recited what was available on the wine list. As I had told no one that I was a struggling alcoholic, I figured this night was an opportune time to have a glass of wine. I followed my new friend's cue, enjoying only one glass. As an alcoholic I try to gauge what is a "normal" drinking pace by those around me. If she would have had three glasses of wine, I would have had three glasses of wine and probably encouraged a fourth. But with only one glass to wet my lips, I eased into our dinner comfortably and we sat and reflected on our UN experience over our candlelit meal. I stared at the swans floating upon the lake. Life was so beautiful in Geneva.

Life was beautiful elsewhere. Away from myself. I wanted to drink more.

Soon, it was time to travel home. On the plane ride, I felt safe enough to indulge in two glasses of red wine. I mean, I had to—the wine was completely free and it didn't make sense not to drink free wine on a plane while flying over Europe. Remember what I said? Hopeless romantic. After the second glass I had to stop because I was too scared of losing control somewhere over the Atlantic Ocean.

I returned home with a momentary high, but I'd come back to my skeletons and they had dug my grave for me in my absence. I didn't know how to live this way. I didn't know how to be honourable and serious and sober. And I didn't know how to ask for help.

Within five days of returning, I was back to drinking and drugging. I would talk about the schools we built, I talked about how we delivered testimony to the United Nations—as if the very mention of these things could redeem me. Then I sat on a couch doing blow for the third night in a row without sleep. I clutched onto these stories as if they bought me the credibility I needed to be worthy of inhabiting my skin. They seemed like memories that no longer belonged to me. I was broken.

"I can only imagine a place like that," Kat said.

"Yeah, it was something else," I said, shifting in the passenger seat as my body tried to contract.

seven

WHEN WE FINALLY GOT TO KAT'S HOUSE, PEOPLE I didn't know were sitting in her living room. They stopped what they were doing to look up at me. I felt like a wild zoo animal on display as Kat led me to her bedroom.

"Just sleep for a while, and I'll check in on you," she instructed me.

Sleep I did. I slept for almost eighteen hours in the safety and comfort of her bed only to be awakened when she brought me a plate of food and a glass of water. Two eggs. Thick bacon. Multigrain toast. I didn't feel like eating but realized that my body needed some form of sustenance. I forced myself to eat. Half an egg. Bite of toast. All the bacon.

That's when I noticed I had messages on my phone. One of them was from my friend Kyla. She had looked out for me on that first trip to Nicaragua. She was doing it again.

"There's a doctoring ceremony on a nearby rez. You've tried everything. I think you should go, I will come there and take you."

I had nothing left to lose. I texted back.

Ok. Let's go.

Kyla had made this suggestion once before. It was a couple of weeks before I'd disappeared to Edmonton, as we stood at our usual lookout point. A quiet perch on a hilltop that we frequented. A place for reflection. It overlooked the Peace River. We always went to that lookout point to talk about life, boys, books, and, more often than not, my affair with booze and blow.

"Kyla," I had confessed to her while standing on top of a picnic table, "I have two roads in front of me right now if I can't sober up. Either I'm going to kill myself or I'm going to fucking disappear."

Kyla went silent for a moment. "Did you ever think of going to see a Medicine Man?" she asked.

"Sometimes I feel like there's a darkness that follows me. Like it has attached itself to me, and I don't think it'll ever leave me alone. Yeah, I've thought about seeing one . . . but Kyla . . ."

"Yeah?"

"We don't know any Medicine Men."

We both started laughing and shook our heads.

Within the span of a few weeks, my world had shifted. And now she knew someone who had access to the medicine world close to Edmonton. It was meant to be.

It didn't surprise me that Kyla got in her car and immediately came to see me. She did it without hesitation the moment she knew I was somewhere safe. She was loyal and loving in a way that I sometimes didn't deserve.

I stood in Kat's driveway anxiously awaiting Kyla's arrival. I could hardly wait to see her beautiful brown face with its sharp Cree features. We have been friends since I was fifteen years old. She has seen me, and loved me, at my lowest. After nights where I had slept with men in a drunken stupor and felt my skin riddled with shame in the morning sun, it was she who'd tell me it would be okay. That I would be okay. That we would make it.

We had a falling out only once. It happened when I became pregnant with my son. She disconnected from me completely, saying I would lose myself by having a baby. She tried to apologize a few weeks later, but I shut her out. All of our bridges were burned and we navigated our waters alone.

Until a year and a half later. We met randomly in a grocery store parking lot and our eyes spoke of mourning. We missed each other and we rebuilt the bridges stronger than before. Before that disagreement, we were young girls weaving our way through our madness. Now we were women. We were sisters.

I think she made a vow to never abandon me again. This is what moved her to drive eight hours to rescue me from my own mess, against her family's wishes, and take me to a ceremony.

She had a worried look on her face as she pulled in to the driveway. After only seconds of us seeing each other, she jumped out of the car and threw her arms around me. We hugged each other tightly. The motion of her body told me that she was crying, and instead of crying too, I absorbed the weight of her sadness.

"That was fuckin' scary, Helen," she said before she let me go. "I thought we lost you for good."

I squeezed her shoulders and let go of her, unable to fully acknowledge that I'd hurt her too when I disappeared. I had to ease myself into feeling emotions.

We put my plastic shopping bag of belongings in the vehicle. She reached into the trunk to grab a jacket that my mom had sent for me. I hugged Kat and she wished me luck before I disappeared down the driveway and toward a journey I wasn't yet sure I was capable of. Kyla's plan meant going back to Edmonton, which wasn't far away. The next day we would head out to the reserve where the ceremony would take place.

We drove and Kyla asked questions I only had short answers to. She turned up the music and I stared out the window at the almost absent Alberta hills.

Kyla had met a guy awhile back who was learning how to become a Road Man, the person who runs the peyote ceremonies. The one we would be going to would be specifically for doctoring.

"You know, I just never thought of him when we talked about taking you to see a Medicine Man. Probably because

Edmonton is so far away. Kinda works out that you ended up here, eh?" she said. I nodded.

Maybe going to this ceremony was what Creator planned. It would give me strength. Maybe Kyla was right. I agreed to meet him.

THE CEREMONY WASN'T until the following day, so we spent that night in a hotel. I showered and became somewhat presentable.

"Want to go to the casino in a bit?" Kyla asked.

"I don't know if that's a good idea," I said.

"We can just go for a little bit, and if you're uncomfortable we can leave," she replied.

I nodded my head. I always agreed to things normal people thought should be easy for me even when I knew that they weren't.

When we got to where all the slots were calling, I could feel the angst rising in my body. Panic, really. It happened sometimes when I found myself in a location where there were many people and liquor was present. Anxiety attacks. Feeling them approach was like hearing thunder in the distance and knowing that soon it could be shaking the very foundations of my house.

It is a dangerous place to be in. My one cousin would try to kill herself when she got like that. Her thunder would come and she would reach for car door handles and try to throw herself out of the vehicle at 120 kilometres an hour.

My hands started shaking like the last leaf clinging to an autumn tree. The one that the slightest breeze threatened to blow off.

My. Body. Screamed.

Need. A. Drink.

Kyla suggested that we eat before we play any games. We had supper and I felt like a child who wanted to eat dessert first. I asked her if she would be angry if I ordered a beer. I cited my shaking hands as cause to do so. I needed it. It was a biological need by this time. My body craved substance.

It was a weak argument but seemed justifiable in the moment.

"No, dude, I would definitely be mad at you," she said blankly from across the table.

I hung my head low and awkwardly changed the subject. I was ashamed of myself and my addictive need. Normal people always expect you to be capable of normal-people things. I had no business being anywhere in public and definitely not where liquor was served. After dinner, I walked in and out between the slot machines trying to think of ways I could sneak a drink and not get caught. If I ordered a rye and Coke at the far side and drank it as fast as I could, I could go undetected, like I have before.

But then I would only have one drink, and one drink would never do. I concocted a get-Helen-drunk plan in my head. Without Kyla knowing, I could go to the store outside and buy a flask, hide that, then get a drink and save the flask for the hotel bathroom. Here at the casino, I could still drink undetected. It couldn't be obvious that I was drinking. I could ask for my drink in the large glasses so it looked like I ordered pop. It wouldn't be obvious that I was drinking.

I could do it.

My hands shook as I pressed the *Repeat Bet* button on the slot machine. I rubbed them against my upper thigh. I didn't know how to stop.

I found Kyla at a slot machine. She was trying to get the fans to line up and give her a feature play. I let her know that I needed to go.

"I can't be here," I said, staring at the floor.

"Okay, I'm losing on this friggin' thing anyways. Let's bounce," she said as she pressed the cash-out button.

I walked silently beside her, the anxiety rising in my chest as we weaved our way through crowds and buzzing machines. When we got to the vehicle, Kyla's phone buzzed and she glanced down.

"It's Max," she said, "He said we leave in the morning but he wants us to come over for a quick visit." Max is the man who would be taking us to ceremony.

"For what?" I asked.

"To talk about what to expect tomorrow."

So, she took me to meet Max. It was why she had driven all that way to get me. I started dreading the introduction the moment we left the casino. Max's clean, sober eyes will know me, I thought. They will know me and they will judge me. We pulled up to his apartment. I felt shame and looked off to the side when Max shook my hand. He was a lot younger than I had expected and couldn't have been much older than I was. He spoke like an Elder, though, and wisdom exuded from his words. I stared out the window while he talked to us.

"There's nothing to be afraid of, and truly you are here for a reason. Don't think it was coincidence, because it isn't," Max started, his voice soft and soothing like a warm blanket on a cold northern winter's evening.

Max continued to explain the process of the peyote ceremony. He instructed me on how and when I would offer my tobacco for my prayers at the beginning. We talked more about my addiction. I explained how I felt that something dark has followed me since I was a teenager. I told him that I was afraid it had come back. I rambled on about how I feared this presence at times and how it made me fearful of my dreams. Max nodded. He didn't look at me like I was delusional.

Even though, so many times, I was convinced that I was. Memory took me back at that very moment.

I WAS SEVENTEEN, and after a weekend of drinking, I lay in my basement bedroom trying to calm my body down enough to sleep. Reality cut in and out. I tossed and turned and then I heard a voice calling to me.

"Helen . . ." It came from inside my head but somewhere else at the same time.

The voice got louder.

"Helen . . ."

My body felt paralyzed. I feared whatever belonged to this voice. To describe it I can only say I felt as though my spirit was being moved from my body forcefully, as if it was being sucked upwards, and I knew that whatever this thing was, it wanted to take over my body or take my spirit. Neither result being one that I wanted, I thrashed inside my body and it was much like I was being held down by invisible restraints.

Then I began to pray. I prayed fiercely and screamed out, "Jesus, help me!" The feeling stopped. My spirit returned to my body and I could move my quivering limbs again. It took me a few minutes to muster up the courage to move. When I finally did, I bolted upstairs and jumped into bed with my mother. I gave thanks for the safety of her embrace and I cried.

Maybe it was the side effects of withdrawing from alcohol. That is what I tried to convince myself. But I've always been aware of a darkness that lurks within addiction. My one auntie told me that she stopped drinking as a teenager. Once she saw a dark presence in a bar. She watched it hover over a man and after he drank enough drinks to get drunk it disappeared into him. Hell, I don't know if it was a story she told me just to keep me sober but I believed her. Still, it wasn't enough to keep me away from the drink.

I've heard similar stories of bad spirits influencing. My dad tells a story about a man in a white Cadillac. He says the man picked up two of my hitchhiking relatives in the middle of the night. This man seemed to know all about them and told them they could have what they wanted. To one man, this stranger promised that he would get his kids back. He promised that they would not be taken from him again. To the other he promised that he could be drunk every day for the rest of his life. He told him that he would never go without liquor again. The man told them he only wanted one thing from them. He never mentioned what that one thing was.

Dude was definitely after some souls that night.

After he sufficiently freaked the fuck out of the both of them, he dropped them off in town at a gas station. As they walked away from the gleaming Cadillac, they glanced back. But there was nothing there. The white car and strange man had disappeared completely.

It woke them up. The one who was promised liquor smartened his ass up shortly after that. He has been sober ever since. The other? I don't know if his path led him back to another encounter or not.

When you're Native, there are many stories like this. Stories of things that occupy Mother Earth.

The Little People.

The hooved man and the "man" who shapeshifts into a dog.

Possessions.

The tall dark spirits and other unexplainable things.

Stories we share as we confirm their presence across territories and mountain ranges.

Stories that tell us there is more to this world than meets the eye.

The idea and reality of hostile and non-human beings roaming the world is not a foreign concept. These stories are not spoken as fables. They are told as real-life stories that were experienced by families and people I know.

I have felt the presence of something unnatural. It's why I felt like something was indulging in my addiction.

A dark thing.

It wanted me.

All of me.

It's why I fear the darkness.

IT WAS DIFFICULT for me to be honest with a stranger after so much time putting up a false front. After we wrapped up our discussion with Max, Kyla and I returned to our hotel room. We were getting ready to watch a movie called *Machine Gun Preacher*, but before we hit play, I talked to my mom on the phone. She begged me to really be careful and urged me not to go to this ceremony.

I was raised with the knowledge of the darkness and yet I was told that Native spiritual practices are evil. It's what the Church taught. I was raised to fear any Native spiritual beliefs. It wasn't Christian. All these heathen practices will only get you sick, hurt, or haunted, or will land you in hell. These were lies that my mom and dad still believed.

Mom pleaded that I pray to what she knew as her God.

The only Native influence I had was when my dad would tell us stories at night about young braves and Indian maidens. He started telling these stories after the time he sat my two brothers and me down in a row: One little, two little, three little . . . Indians, he told us.

We were Indians.

We all began to cry and whine and plead as if our objections could pin down our blood line and make it say uncle.

Grandfather.

I am not of your blood.

My brother raised his hand when Dad told us we were Indians, and through the tears in his eyes he asked our father, "But we're still part human, right?"

This prompted my father to start telling these stories, and they helped. Dad had to learn some history himself to even have a base of knowledge from which to concoct these tales for us. But they also helped create the idea that Indians existed only in that era of war ponies and teepees. We weren't real. We were a part of history.

We weren't here and living today.

I LIVED IN a house and we went to church every Sunday. Dad preached sometimes. Mom made big dinners. We took Sunday drives on dirt roads you could travel miles down only to have to come back again. We didn't talk much about being Indian. I didn't even know what kind of Indian I was. The idea of being Indian was very much like saying I had brown hair, ten toes, and two ears. It was a feature.

It was a fact.

As I got older, I became more interested in our cultural traditions, and in fourth grade I went to one of the functions for all of the Native kids from across the school district. It was time that I checked out what this Native culture was all about. Our group worked really hard preparing the gift we would take to trade with another group. I made a dream catcher with baby-blue edging and multicoloured pony beads. Almost every Native kid ends up making a dream catcher in school, but probably less than one-third of them might be from the tribe where it originates from. I thought it was the prettiest thing ever until I received my trade, which was a little burgundy medicine bag, and then I thought *it* was the prettiest thing ever. The neck strands were decorated with a pretty pattern of beads, and it had some small unidentifiable animal painted on the front. I decided it was a wolf. Wolves were my mother's favourite animal. I was smitten with it and couldn't wait to go home and show my parents. I flew into the house, already clutching my medicine bag, eager to show my father, who was sitting at the table.

"Daddy! Daddy!" I cried out.

"What is it, princess?" he asked, looking up from the newspaper.

"Look what I got today. A whole bunch of us Native students met together, Daddy! We pretended we were different tribes and—"

"What is it?" my father interrupted me.

"It's a medicine bag," I replied.

My father grabbed the medicine bag from my hands. I watched him with curiosity and then horror when I realized he was headed for the garbage.

"What are you doing!?" I shrieked in my small girl voice.

My father opened the lid of the garbage and tossed the medicine bag in. I stood in the kitchen crying. I learned that there was something deeply wrong with being an Indian.

"That stuff is bad. All of it. BAD!" he barked at me. Then he sat down and resumed reading his paper.

I ran up to my room and cried. I didn't understand and he offered no explanation. Later that year, when all the other Native kids got to go on an overnight cultural camp, I was not allowed to go. My parents' actions further solidified the forming belief that being an Indian was bad.

It wasn't until years later that my dad told me one of the main reasons he distrusted Native spirituality and ways of being. He said that the mother who raised him, the one I am named after, was very sick and they decided to take her to a Medicine Man. He wasn't able to help her, and she died immediately after. Dad said he didn't know much about this other world. About the world of spirit, medicine, and ceremony. So, when his mom died he turned his finger to the Medicine Man. The event gave him a place to put all of his blame for the loss of his mom.

There was a period of time when I was a teenager that my dad suffered from an unexplainable illness. He would go into random coughing fits until he blacked out. This started happening more and more frequently. The fits would hit when he was driving. He would wake to find himself in the ditch. Unscathed but rattled. The fainting spells would hit him when he was standing. He'd just fall over without warning, dropping like an old giant tree to the ground. Thirty seconds later, he would be as alert as a morning bird. But it was getting to the point that we feared for his life. He sought advice from many doctors and they ran tests on him but no one could figure out why this was happening.

One time, while the two of us were sitting in Dairy Queen together, a fit hit him hard. I got up to stand beside him, knowing a blackout would follow. I watched my dad's eyes roll back. Ice cream melted and dripped from the corner of his mouth as I caught him and held him up in his seat. The people eating their burgers and ice creams panicked and a few of them rushed to our table.

"Do we need to call an ambulance?" one guy said loudly. His eyes were wide and frantic.

"No, it's okay," I said. "He just does this sometimes."

As if on cue, Dad came back to consciousness. He shook his head gruffly, then resumed eating his ice cream. The guy who'd offered to help looked confused and walked back to his table.

After Dad exhausted all avenues of healing, with no luck, he went to a Medicine Man. The healer talked about some quilts my dad had recently purchased from someone. How that man knew is a mystery. No one had mentioned the blankets. But my dad did buy them and the Medicine Man said something in the blankets was causing the trouble. He said someone had put something bad in the fibre of those quilts. Medicine designed to make my dad sick. He told my dad that he needed to burn those blankets.

Dad took his advice and burned those blankets that very night. After that, he was fine. He was healthy again. What my father had blamed for taking his mother from him had saved his own life.

eight

SO MANY MEMORIES PLAYED IN MY HEAD THE ENTIRE
time that Kyla and I watched that movie in the hotel. *Machine
Gun Preacher*. I loved that the name was a mix of badassery
and faith. Even bad men find redemption. Even good men
lose their way. One thing was for sure: I was safe here. We
were sober. And when the show ended, I thought about the
main character. He had such an unshakable faith in God, in
Jesus. It caused me to worry. Was going to a traditional healer
and ceremony not believing in the God I had known? Could
I be hurt? Was I turning my back on the God whom I was
raised to believe in? The generational paranoia of my own
cultural practices rattled my already shaken mind and heart.

There were times over the past few months where I had
emptied myself into prayer. In the darkness of my room,
I had asked Jesus and God to help me. I had felt helpless.

I cried and curled into the fetal position in my hotel room that night. The moonlight that streamed in provided enough light that I could still see myself. I still existed. But I was fading fast.

We were going to leave the city with Max tomorrow morning.

The universe brought me to this point. I was supposed to meet Max. I needed to go to the ceremony, but I was raised Christian. It all conflicted with my upbringing.

But then again, so did excessive drug use.

Max greeted me as a friend when we finally arrived at his apartment the following day. We ate, we chatted, and we rested. But there was still a gnawing. Something uncomfortable.

It was sometime in that early morning darkness, before we had left for Max's place, that I decided not to go to the ceremony—even though it was the reason we had stayed in the city. Kyla didn't argue. She understood and honoured my decision when I told her. I am sure she was a little nervous herself about the whole thing.

I was going to say thank you to Max. I wanted him to know I appreciated his offer but I was not able to go, that I felt conflicted inside. I just couldn't get rid of the guilt that I'd be turning away from God if I went to this doctoring ceremony. I decided to wait outside the apartment while Kyla visited a bit more. I called my son and lit a cigarette.

He needed to know that I loved him and that I would be back soon.

I could hear his tiny voice on the other end of the line and I asked him if he wanted to go to Vancouver on a trip with me. An organization that I was involved with had extended an offer to travel for another project. They knew I was a single mom and said they'd arrange to take both me and my son. I thought the trip would be good for us. Getting away would bring us closer. Heal some wounds.

Instead, I heard indecision in his small voice. Distrust and words that treated me like a stranger. He did not want to go with me. He did not trust me anymore, and I couldn't blame him. In that moment, I knew I could not return home still broken and half a person.

I would do it.

My beautiful son's voice made me change my mind. I would become healed for him and for myself. My love for Mathias trumped questions of the faith I had known. It cancelled out what the Church has taught. I could no longer afford to be scared of anything that could help me become whole.

I went back inside Max's apartment and I could hear him in the other room singing to himself as he packed what he needed to get ready for the ceremony. Kyla looked up at me from the couch.

"So how did it go?" she asked, wondering about my conversation with Mathias.

"I changed my mind. We're going to ceremony," I said, and she nodded, happy to know I was taking this step.

Within twenty minutes, we were outside of city limits driving in a direction I had never been. We were headed to a reserve I had never heard of. I watched the sea of pale gold canola fields sway in the wind. I drifted in and out of the conversation about the medicine: Peyote. I had never heard of it.

I was scared because I knew that there would be older people at this gathering. I knew they'd be able to take one look at me and—know things. They would be able to see straight through my bullshit and into the dark place I was living. There is no hiding from people who know things. The nervousness built up in my chest and I receded into myself when we got to the house. I didn't have any shirts except for tank tops. I knew from attending a Sweat Lodge once that I needed to dress modestly and have my shoulders covered. Max lent me one of his extra shirts that he had in the trunk of his car. It was a black shirt with Kermit the Frog on the front and big white lettering that read "Something smells green in here."

We pulled up to a faded yellow house, and a young Native guy with two braids was outside having a smoke. There were two other vehicles in the driveway and I knew we were early. As we made our way inside, I nodded at the young man while Max gave him a hug. I could smell the sweetgrass being burned somewhere in the house and heard laughter coming from up the stairs. I took a deep breath, grabbed the wooden banister, and followed behind Kyla and Max. There were a few Elders peppered across the living room and a woman busying herself in the kitchen. I scanned the walls and looked at the family pictures. There was one of those wooden picture frames with spaces for school pictures from kindergarten to Grade 12 but half of the slots were missing a photo. My kohkum had a lot of those same frames filled with pictures of her other grandkids. I sat on the floor beside an Elder who was wearing a baseball cap and a blue-and-white-striped button-up.

"Where you from?" he asked me.

"Fort St. John. I'm Dane Zaa and Cree," I replied.

"Oh, from up over that-a-way?"

"Yes," I answered as I stared off, not wanting to make eye contact.

"Here I was going to ask if you were from further in BC."

"Why's that?"

"Your shirt. I thought you were from the Frog Clan," he said slyly.

The Elders around the room howled and one piped in, "You'll see! Maybe you'll hear them frogs croakin' tonight during ceremony."

"Just might if you listen real hard," the baseball-capped one said.

My face went red. I let out a fake laugh but I was unhappy about being the centre of attention. I sat on the floor as more people arrived, some travelling from great distances to be there. I watched them interact and answered in short, stoic sentences when spoken to. As the preparations for ceremony began, I helped. I busied myself moving furniture when instructed, sweeping floors, and picking up wayward toddlers who scurried about.

As the evening progressed, it was clear the circle was ready. But I was not—even though I was still sitting there participating. The ceremony was about to begin and I had no idea what to expect. It made me want to bolt in fear. Not knowing what to expect. But I couldn't leave. Not this time. I eased my worry by telling myself this was the night for new beginnings.

Ceremony began.

The experience was one of the scariest nights of my life. Mostly because of mistaken belief—things I'd been told. It was also the night of a new beginning for me. I experienced many things sitting there in the house meeting with the fifteen or so other people. I could feel the sickness in my spirit coming out of my pores. It reminded me of when I had food poisoning. My sickness was real and it was pouring out of me. I had to close my eyes and focus on prayer the entire time because I was worried of losing my grip on reality. The funny thing is, in order to fully trust the medicine I had to lose my grip on reality.

Around midnight, there were a few minutes where people could go outside and have a smoke or stretch their legs as the ceremony continued inside. I broke prayer to watch a handful of people trickle out and I wanted to leave with them. I wanted desperately to leave with them. I needed to take a moment of fresh air. I needed to have a break from the intensity of weaving in and out of reality. But then I realized that if I went outside, I would not want to come back in. And then I would find myself outside and alone in the dark. Lost on the rez, on peyote. Nope. Not today. I stayed with the people at the ceremony. I closed my eyes tight and began to pray again.

I won't say much about that night because it is deeply personal and sacred. I will say that the medicine told me and showed me how to treat and respect it. It showed me how to focus on prayer and to understand that as a medicine it wasn't to be approached like some hallucinogenic. The medicine told me to respect it. This is not metaphorical. It told me. I listened. I prayed intensely. I had to fight barriers and guards that wanted to keep the medicine out and hold it back from doing its job. I could actually feel the struggle inside of me to release and let go. Once, I fought the darkness and allowed for spirit to rise—I saw a bright white light and images came.

Right there in that living room where the ceremony was being held, I heard an eagle cry, as though it were right beside me. I kept praying.

After the ceremony ended, the next morning, we headed home. None of us—Kyla, Max, or I—had slept all night. The lack of sleep didn't bother me. My mind was finally clear. I felt a sense of peace for the first time in a long time. My mind wasn't rattling off at a million miles per minute. I had forgotten how light it felt to not obsess about my addiction or alcoholism. It was a clarity that I cherished.

But only for a few moments. That's because my brain started its addict monologue, though a little quieter this time. I sat in the passenger seat fearful of fucking things up. I prayed some more and the quiet returned.

During the drive, and after a long silence in the back seat, I finally spoke. "That eagle cry was so loud, hey?"

"What eagle cry?" Max asked.

"Yeah right—you guys had to have heard it too. It was loud, it sounded like the eagle was right in the middle of the room," I said.

"No, man, I didn't hear it either," Kyla said from the passenger seat.

"You have a gift, Helen. That was a gift," Max said from the front seat.

I sat silently again, wondering what the eagle's visit meant. I knew the spirit of an eagle came down to help me heal. I was grateful for the visit. I was humbled. We went back to Max's house and then Kyla and I hopped in Kyla's car and started on the eight-hour drive home.

As the sun set that day, Kyla and I pulled the car over and took a short break. We walked into a prairie field. We laid tobacco and gave thanks.

That night I sought comfort from haklay eenzah, *Grandmother Moon*, and suhn, *the stars*. I was tired of my outbursts, weary of my wandering, and frustrated with my faithlessness. I gazed upwards from the passenger seat, asking them to watch over me at night and guide my footsteps so that I will travel a good path. I told those in the spirit world that I no longer wanted to harm myself or those whom I love. I asked that they continue to help me.

A minute after my prayer to the night sky, Kyla and I witnessed the largest shooting star either of us had ever seen. It blazed a path ahead of us, leaving behind a mesmerizing stream. I offered up my thanks, humbled by the acknowledgement. My prayers were heard.

Before this moment, I knew that Grandmother Moon had witnessed my self-destruction for far too long. I hadn't allowed her to intervene. Her feminine spirit was only able to empower me with the ability to cleanse myself through moon times. Does this sacred time still hold its power to cleanse and renew if we neither acknowledge it nor understand its meaning? I wonder if she wanes overhead with sorrow as she watches us, her granddaughters, forget our power. As we forget who we really are. Forget our beauty. Become blind to our worth.

But there she is, ever-present, the grandmother who waits for us to remember.

My asu is born of the Dane Zaa tribe. She is blessed with skin the colour of the deep soil of Mother Earth and hair black like ravens' wings. She has never failed to mirror my potential back to me when I was unable to see it. My asu's praying hands, weathered, wrinkled, and cracked, speak of hardships held and burdens carried. These arthritic, aged hands move purposefully and are capable of swift but gentle gestures. With the same beautiful brown fingers that count rosary beads, she has cradled my face and raised my eyes to meet hers. In that gaze lives the warmth of a thousand home fires. Acceptance I could not give myself. And the strength of a love to which I had blinded myself.

In the physical absence of a blessed matriarch, we need only look to Grandmother Moon.

The constant light within the darkness. The grandmothers who came before us. Although they are unseen, they remain connected to us. They always help us remember who we are. Our grandmothers are undoubtedly a part of us and their knowledge and teachings are still accessible. Especially to those who are thirsty and willing to drink of their wisdom and knowledge.

I am trying to remember my sacredness.

I am trying to remember who I am.

I am trying to remember my grandmothers.

THAT NIGHT, I slept in my own bed, awakening to the sound of the water drum streaming into the room from somewhere unseen. The spirit world was calling. My eyes scanned the room to see an old Native woman with long hair watching over me. She was standing in the corner. But this time, I wasn't scared of her. I looked at her, smiled, and went back to sleep.

In the morning, my four-year-old son ran into the room. I pulled him into the bed beside me and held him tightly in my grateful arms. I held my tears back as we lay in bed and talked. It had been too long since we'd shared a moment like this.

Mommy was home.

Part Two
The In-Between

nine

MY FAMILY HAS A STRONG AND PROUD HISTORY. LIFE though? Life in this colonial state has been our great unknowing.

We are born knowing and trusting who we are.

Blood memories.

That ancient knowledge of those who came before me navigates my veins. It moves with purpose, like the birchbark canoes of my ancestors moved swiftly down the Sikanni River. I was born knowing things. I was born with a connection to earth, to water, and to animals.

I was born to dream.

My great-great-grandfather was Chief Makanecha, or, as the white man interpreted it, Chief Bigfoot. Makanecha signed Treaty 8 in 1911. In 1910, when the Treaty commissioners first tried to engage him and other Dane Zaa in the immediate territory, my grandfather replied, "God made the game and fur-bearing animals for the Indians, and money for the white people. My forefathers made their living in the country without white men's money. My people can do the same."

Auntie told me that he had waited to sign to see if the white men would hold their promises and to make sure that our people would remain free and not be stuck on reserves. Our people were the last to sign a Treaty. I have heard that they left us to last because they hoped we would die off and they wouldn't have to deal with us.

Bigfoot was sought out in the mountains by many when hard times struck. They would ask him to pray over an item of hide or cloth and it would become a prayer flag. A sacred item used to alter events for the better. I have heard stories of him being a healer of sorts.

When I was in my twenties, Asu told me the story of when the diseases finally caught up to our people.

"A few of them went off to hunt," she said as she carved their trail with her finger in the air. "When they finally came back they were going to come down the hill to where the people were camped." Again she moved her hands, sculpting out the valley. "One person seen them coming and yelled to them, 'Turn around! A sickness has come and everybody is dying here. Turn around!'"

Asu stopped at this part for a few moments. The look in her eyes told me she had transported herself to another place and time that even her old eyes had not seen. It was still very real for her.

"So, what could they do? They had no choice but to leave their family and all those people behind to die. There used to be so many of us before. So many . . ." her voice trailed off. Her sadness was palpable.

We are a small tribe, well under three thousand. One can only imagine how many more of us there would be if not for the sicknesses that decimated the population.

These stories settle in the bones. It doesn't matter that these stories happened a long time ago. It matters because it happened to us—to my people. The grief is real. So is the loss.

I sometimes wonder if Bigfoot would have signed the Treaty at all, though, if he could see what has happened over the past few decades. If he saw our life now and how our territory has been ripped up by roads, the landscape spotted with oil and gas wells, the rivers dammed like blocked arteries, would he have disappeared back in to the mountains and refused the Treaty? And how would Bigfoot react if he saw our people struggling, witnessed the addictions and the suicides? Would he weep and pray if he knew that so many have gotten lost and have forgotten who they are and where they came from?

I was told he helped push wagons off the Peace River Valley cliffs. It was a protest of the encroaching settlers who had begun taking up all of the game. Some people may see that and see a "savage." I see it and see someone protecting his people and doing so the way he knew how.

I come from resistance and strength.

His son was my great-grandpa Charlie Bigfoot, who married Nina Chipesia. They were Asu's parents. Asu's name is June Bigfoot. She had a brother named John and a sister named Mary. When Asu was small, her mother passed away and her father was gone into the mountains. That's when the Indian agents came.

At first they wanted to send Asu and her siblings away to a residential school but Grandpa downright refused. Asu was raised by another family as their own. Her father visited when he could after coming back from hunts and trading intermittently.

The times of change had already started taking shape on the people and their interactions with one another. Asu gets lost in story often. Her body becomes a living portrait of the past as she carves out geography in the air with her finger, or her hand becomes a fist to mimic a turning head.

"I had a little sister," she told me once. "I didn't even know but that's probably how my mom died. I went into a room and that baby was laying there. I picked her up and held her." Asu shifted her arms to hold an imaginary baby and began to rock it.

"*Baby*," she cooed, rocking the air. "But the baby didn't move. There was something wrong with it. I called again. *Baby*. Nothing. She was dead."

After my grandmother told me this story, we lay beside each other and cried. I held her fragile aging body, ravaged by diabetes.

Asu continued to tell stories.

"They called me a bastard as I walked behind the Indian agents when they went to bury my mom. I was just a little girl. I remember them saying I was an ugly bastard who doesn't even know her mother is dead. They said that," Asu tells me the story that she has told me countless times before. It's in moments like this that I wish I could build a canoe that would cross time. I would paddle back and rescue her.

But there were good times too.

Asu told me that when she was older, she would trail off into the bushes by herself with a book and tea kettle in hand. She would spend hours reading wherever she made her fire. They still lived in seasonal camps up until the 1950s. After that, the area where Asu lived and travelled became known as Indian Reservation 4. It didn't take long before she wasn't allowed to freely wander on the land anymore. The construction of the Alaska Highway opened up the territory to more settlers, creating access. The landscape began to change slowly at first, and then one day they built a day school. Our families were expected to no longer be nomadic so their children could attend school.

But the settlers' presence meant other new things for Asu. She tells me stories about her father returning from hunting or trading and bringing with him oranges and sweets for all the kids. Asu's auntie, Bella, was introduced to western-style dancing and tried to do the "twist" dance move while Grandpa Jumbie was drumming. This was during a tea dance, a dance that is about praying. When Grandpa Jumbie saw Bella trying to twist down to the ground like she saw white ladies do, he stopped drumming instantly. "No drumming today," he said as he rose and took his drum with him back to his cabin. Chubby Checker's dance moves had reached the bushes and fires of the Dane Zaa. Change was coming.

Asu has told me stories of Grandma's (Jumbie's wife Margaret) impeccable aim that could knock a grouse out on the first hit and guide an axe swiftly to a fleeing rabbit.

Grandpa Jumbie was the Cree man who raised my asu as his own. He once warned Asu of the things to come and spoke of the things to stay away from. He was a dreamer. He held the ability of knowing. He would dream of the events that would come to pass, some of which could still be prevented.

I am of Dane Zaa blood through my maternal bloodline. I am Métis/Cree through my paternal bloodline. My people dreamt of the future. They dreamt of the hunt and they used the dream world as a channel to navigate to the trail way to heaven. One of my great-grandpa's warnings was to stay away from certain substances that would surely cause a disconnect between us, the dream world, and the trail way to heaven.

"This powder," he said as he traced small lines along the palm of his leathery hand, "will do a lot of harm and cloud your vision."

"This too," he said as he raised his fingers to his mouth, making puffing motions with his lips, "will be no good for our people."

Grandpa continued to describe places where he had never physically been. He spoke of a real darkness that existed in many homes. Many of us heard these warnings too late or not at all. Much of what he said was forgotten and most of us fell into a deep sleep.

But it was a period of sleeping without dreaming.

A tribe of dreamers in the dreamless void.

My dreamless void began early, much too early.

My parents were never fully aware of the magnitude of the sexual abuse that I, and many other of my family members, endured. Both of my parents tried really hard to give us a life that they never had. My father came from a Métis community called Moccasin Flats. He was raised by his kohkum Helen in a house a block away from his two brothers and two sisters.

His brothers and sisters lived with his biological mom, Lillian, and his dad, Jerry. Grandpa Jerry's first home was on a farm. When Grandpa Jerry was still a toddler, his father went off to war and died overseas, leaving his wife and kids to work the land. They struggled with so much land to work all alone. Great-Grandma Mariah was a hard woman with hands that worked just as hard as any man's, but she couldn't perform miracles. They still lost the farm. On top of that, Jerry's father had lost his Treaty Status on account of fighting in the war that ended up getting him killed. This disenfranchisement left his bloodline disconnected from family and community. Giving my great-grandfather the "privileges" of being a citizen and no longer an "Indian" governed by the Indian Act didn't make him or his children white. It just made them lost.

Grandma Lillian was first raised on a big farm with Kohkum Helen and Grandpa Joe. When Grandpa and Kohkum got hitched they had eleven horse carriages at their wedding. They were definitely considered well off. Grandpa Joe wanted to try his hand at being a logger and sold the farm. They moved the family to Moccasin Flats. He never did become a logger. Instead, he became a lean, mean drinking machine, always laying hands to Kohkum. Kohkum, who didn't speak any English, would always tell him that one day he would pay for his actions. He would suffer for it later on in life. And he did pay for it in his old age.

They say that a family that prays together stays together. But what happens when the prayers are sparse? And when liquor seeps into the baseboards and rots the foundation, what happens then?

Grandma Lillian and Grandpa Jerry got together at a young age. They shacked up and started a family. One winter my grandpa had been away for several months on a drinking spree, leaving my grandma to fend for herself and her four kids. At the time, she was pregnant with their fifth. She wiped noses, made fires, cooked, and even managed to find the food so there was something to be cooked. But parenting was a struggle.

Grandma went to residential school. She started having babies at the age of fourteen. Parenting was abstract to her. She had never seen it modelled and she didn't know how to practise. That was just one part of the legacy of residential schools: the denial of the right to be parented by your own parents. It resulted in not knowing how to parent your own children. To this day, Grandma still has night terrors. That place haunted her for an entire lifetime. This inability to parent is just one small fraction of the negative impacts of the residential school. It continues to affect three generations of my family.

Residential schools and policies aimed at eradicating the Indian broke Indian spirits. Broke hopes and dreams. Broke smiles before lips could turn up. And they almost broke my family completely.

Yet Grandma did the best she could with what she had been given. She arranged for another family a few hours away to come and take my dad, who was still in diapers. There was too much to be done and something had to change. It just so happened to be Dad who would be the one who had to do the changing. All of those children and a missing husband made the sweat from Grandma's brow a little harder to wipe off. Word of my father's pending adoption travelled fast, and one night, Kohkum walked into Grandma's house. A tornado of snowflakes was chasing her. She looked at my grandma, who was peeling potatoes, and then looked at my father, who was sitting on the floor crying with snot running down his face.

"That one," Kohkum said, pointing her finger at my dad. "I came to take that one."

My grandma only nodded her head and resumed peeling her potatoes as Kohkum grabbed Dad and bundled him in the patchwork blanket that she brought for him. She took him outside in the blistering cold and plopped him into

an old wooden toboggan. That is how he came to live with
Kohkum. He grew up in a small two-bedroom shack with
eighteen other people. At night they would line up like
sardines on the living room floor, elbow to elbow. There
was no room to dream in a house like that.

My father would go and visit his family, never quite
understanding why he wasn't living with them. He hungered
for their acceptance. He was banned from the house because
he would eat their food. Grandma's home had food in the
cupboards that Kohkum couldn't afford. They had oranges.
They had cookies. His siblings would be on the other side
of the door as he would try to push his way in.

"Noooo!!" his sister once yelled at him through the door.
"If I let you in, I will get in trouble. We aren't *allowed* to
let *you* in!"

He stood on the other side of the door, shoulders slumped
in defeat. His siblings would line up at the window, their
brown faces staring at him through the glass as if he were
some strange animal at a zoo. The separation was not just a
walk down the road. A real, emotional, and nurturing line
that Dad could never cross was created the winter night
that Kohkum took him away.

There is evidence of disconnection of a displaced people
everywhere. Dad witnessed men in the community beating
their wives as if it were ritual. He witnessed families drinking
themselves into oblivion and back.

Later, when he was finally allowed back in his family's
house, he was made to fight his brother in the living room.

My grandpa and his drunken friends would jeer them on. "Hit him again!" they would yell as the boys pummelled each other. Both boys were scared because if they stopped too early, their father would lay a beating on them. A brown belt, clutched by a father's brown hand, was always in their periphery. The blood of brothers had to be drawn.

Years later, when Dad would tell me this story, he said he always won those fights. He asked his brother decades later, grown man to grown man, if he hated him for it. My father, who has repeated this story without emotion a thousand times, became teary-eyed when he said his brother told him no, he didn't hate him. They did what they had to do. They survived.

There weren't a lot of families with a steady income. Most lived on welfare. The few who did have a steady income could be counted on one hand. My father, raised with this mentality, looked forward to receiving his first welfare cheque—that is, until Kohkum sat him down and set him straight. "Look around you," she told him in Cree. "All of these Indians who live here are on welfare. Not you. I want you to be different. I don't want you to be like these people. Whatever family you get, I want you to work hard for your family."

When Dad was a little boy, the owner of the land on which Moccasin Flats sat sold the land from right under their sleeping heads. None of the town's people wanted half-breeds near the town. The family couldn't have afforded to live in town anyway. Because they weren't "Indian" anymore, they couldn't very well move back to a reserve. They were the dispossessed and the displaced.

But not everyone in town was hard-hearted.

The mayor of Chetwynd at the time was Frank Oberle. He took up the plight of the people of Moccasin Flats and headed to Ottawa. That mayor secured a chunk of funding from the federal government. When he came back, he hired the Métis to help build their own houses. By the time my dad was a teenager, everyone was living in these identical houses with warped cement basements. They renamed this new place Wabi Crescent, but it quickly became known as Sesame Street. The nickname came about on the account of there being an Oscar, an Ernie, and a woman they called Big Bird living there. Being treated like an interloper, new homes or not, breaks down a man. Trying to secure work in a town that didn't even want you living in it was kinda like trying to haul water from a creek with a bucket that has the bottom broken out of it. You knew it was pointless so you stopped going down to the water at all and stayed thirsty.

So they drank liquor instead.

Or they left to work somewhere an Indian could earn the money his work was worth. Many men had to leave to feed their families. Grandpa Jerry was one of them, and as time went on he earned a name for being one of the best workers in the region.

Sesame Street had only one way in and one way out. It wasn't a place where many white people came to visit. Unless, of course, you count the police. They visited often.

My dad remembers a time when he was eight or nine years old. He and Kohkum had gone to bingo. Little kids always frequented bingo halls and lingered outside of drinking establishments in those days. The bingo hall that the people played at was at the entrance of Sesame Street. That's when officers arrived. They were there to arrest one of Sesame Street's own. A man named Billy who had a three-hundred-dollar outstanding fine. They wanted to take Billy to jail.

"I don't want to go to jail," Billy said to the officers.

"Well, Billy, we gotta take you in," one replied.

"I'll give you two hundred dollars," Billy told them, "and I ain't going to jail."

"Billy, it's too late," the other officer stated sternly. "We are taking you to jail."

Billy jumped up and dashed out the door with the police officers and my dad chasing after him. Dad watched from afar as the cops stood next to their cop car outside of Billy's house. Billy's door flung open and he fired two shots from his gun over the top of the police car. The door shut again, and the two cops talked to each other before jumping on their speaker.

"Billy," said one cop over the speaker, "we will take the two hundred dollars."

Sure enough, Dad said, he watched Billy hand over the money and the two cops left Sesame Street. It was a different place then and operated by its own set of rules. My dad did succeed one time at bringing two white friends home, but first he had to calm their fears of Sesame Street and tell them they weren't going to get shot by a bow and arrow just walking down the road. They reluctantly agreed and visited. Dad laughed as he confirmed that, yes, they made it out alive.

Dad didn't heed Kohkum's words about working right away. In fact, he did the opposite. He stole bikes, then moved up the ladder to car stereos and vehicles, and dealing acid. Dad, a seasoned brawler from living room fights, would go into nearby towns and pummel men just for glancing at him the wrong way. He drank like liquor was his family's redemption. He was a man's man. He was set on making a name for himself and aimed to be the wildest son of a bitch out there. At parties, he would ram his head through walls. He would chew glass, smash beer bottles over his head, and put lit cigarettes out on his tongue. The boys he grew up with were just as crazy. Crazy, broken, and dangerous to handle. They were a loyal pack, like an Indian version of *The Outsiders*, except for they would have kicked the Outsiders' asses in a brawl. But my dad, he did all of this with intention. He planned on killing himself. He wanted to be remembered. This was the only way he knew how to be remembered.

My mom, on the other hand, wanted to be a nun. She spent nights crying and conflicted about whether she should love God more or love her parents more. She loved her parents. She loved God. She loved her parents. She loved God. My little mother wept often.

She grew up as one daughter out of five, in a world where she was never white enough or brown enough. The kids at school called her wagon burner, dirty half-breed, and squaw. Mom learned how to fight hard early on. In Grade 6, during an awards ceremony, her ears perked up when her name was called. She was excited—this was her first award. When she reached the front of the class she was given a small trophy with a broken hockey stick that read "Bully of the Year." She was not proud. Instead, she found the whole ordeal humiliating and said that she fought only when she had to. That just happened to be all the time.

Later, in high school, she tossed a boy straight through a glass window. As she and the boy sat in the principal's office, the boy smirked. It was his taunting of privilege that said, "You fucked up. I'm white and you're not." Surprisingly, the principal was aware of my mother's repeated experiences and knew of the deep racism within the school. And he actually cared. He dismissed Mom and told the boy to come up with the funds to replace the window.

We called my mom's father Papa. He was a white man from Montana with a knack for storytelling. He had a big family and a checkered past that he left behind when he came to Canada. Papa had filled a lot of roles back home but his main one was as his older brother's keeper.

Another drinking story.

Papa and his brother were at a bar in their town, White-fish. Papa ordered a glass of water and snacked on the bowl of nuts on the bar top. His brother decided it was a good time to get completely shitfaced. Anytime was a good time to get completely shitfaced.

Papa, being a young but well-built sixteen-year-old, was his brother's bodyguard and part-time wing man. That night, his brother was feeling particularly mischievous. His drunken master plan was to run out of the bar with the bartender's jar of tip money. The barkeep yelled as he ran out the door. A fellow in the bar took off after him. My papa was calm and ate another nut before casually rising and then exiting to rescue his brother.

Outside, the man had Papa's brother on the ground. He was giving him a good whoopin'. That's when Papa grabbed the man by the collar, lifted him up, and clocked him once. It turned out that he dislocated the man's jaw. And that jaw belonged to the mayor of the town.

MY PAPA WAS sentenced to three years in Deerlodge Prison, where he mastered the craft of making toilet wine and hooch from scrap kitchen items. Potato peels. Bread. Sugar. Fruit. Yeast. He had multiple recipes and made do with whatever he had at the time.

It was near the end of his sentence when something terrifying happened, something that unsettled him right into his old age: the Deerlodge Prison Riot of '59.

A couple of prisoners took over the prison and Papa said that they were scary, evil men. They tied up some of the guards in one of the cells, leaving a gas can in front of them. They were constantly threatening to burn them alive. At the time, Papa was working in the kitchen and even though he was scared, he carried out his daily cooking duties and spent the rest of the time hiding out in his cell. Papa always got a frightened look when he told this story. The memory haunted him. He said the men who started the rampage took to raping some of the younger boys. It was like travelling through hell. Eventually, the National Guard was called in and that was the end of that. All of the men who had taken over the prison were dead by the end of it.

Not long after he got released, Papa decided to set off for Alaska to find work. Instead, he found himself in Fort Nelson. He was really something else. Papa couldn't read or write but he could damn sure put in an honest day's work. He could also build a hell of a lean-to in the bush.

Eventually, he met Asu. They shacked up and began to have children. After a few years they moved the whole family off-reserve and settled in Dawson Creek. When my fair-skinned mother and her four sisters would go to the rez to visit, they would get bugged. They were taunted for being white and "city Indians." Still, there were times on the rez when everyone got along and played games together. When cousins and non-related girls on the rez were like sisters to her. But Mom never felt like she belonged on the rez. Mom never felt like she belonged in town either. The only place she felt like she fit was with her immediate family. Mom. Dad. Sisters. The end. But even belonging in the family was hard.

Asu and Papa were alcoholics. For some reason, they thought it was a good parenting practice to take one of the kids with them when they went to the bar or to another town to party. Usually that kid was my mother. Sometimes it seemed that going was the lesser of two evils, because if she stayed home, her older sisters would pick on her. Besides, she would always get some free treats to bide her time in the vehicle or would be set up in a nearby café. My mother told me a story of a time when she and her sisters were in the vehicle, waiting for their parents.

The stars and the moon were the only ones watching over them. They were a car full of frightened girls. Drunks stumbled by and there was always the odd one who would try to get into the car. The girls realized the only barrier they could create between them and the drunks was one of fog. All of them summoned their breath and exhaled on the windows, creating a temporary cocoon.

Mom had a lot of stories like that.

One time, while her parents were driving away from a party, a man insulted Asu. Through the open passenger window, Mom heard the man call Asu a dirty bitch. Mom was eight years old and flung her little body halfway out that window as she swung her clenched fists wildly at the man. No one was calling her mom a name on her watch. Papa had to hit the gas while Asu pulled her back into the car so that the situation didn't escalate. No one fucks with Bigfoot women. Ever.

Mom was a good girl. She cleaned the house, helped out, cooked a lot of the dinners, and stood up for her sisters. Eventually, my non-wild, rough and tough, wannabe-nun mom met my father. I think she wanted to save him. I think my dad secretly wanted to be saved.

Mom had a lot of suitors but my dad was the only one who had succeeded. At a party, when they were still just acquaintances, my dad walked up and stood in front of another guy who was having a conversation with her. He cut the man off completely and, because my dad already had a name for being a fighter, there was no retaliation. The man scurried away and my father won my mother's attention that first evening. He was relentless and fearless in his pursuit of her.

Shirley Bigfoot was going to be his woman.

SOON AFTER, MY dad and a bunch of the wild boys stayed the night at Asu and Papa's house. It was the first time my father had been in their house. When my dad woke up on the living room floor, Papa was cooking in the kitchen. My dad had no idea his girl had a white man for a father, and he thought, "Who is this white man cooking in the kitchen of these Indian girls' house?"

Convinced that this white man had stumbled in off the street, Dad went and sat at the table and watched him. Papa was making burgers at the stove. My papa didn't stop to say hello to the stray Indian boy watching him. He just carried about his business. He was making food for him and Asu because they were going to go on a drive up the Alaska Highway.

Papa slid a burger onto some bread.

My dad grabbed it and started eating it.

Papa made another burger and slid it onto bread.

My dad grabbed this one and started eating it.

Papa made another burger and slid it onto bread.

My dad reached for it, when my papa finally barked, "Quit eating all my burgers, ya asshole!"

This is how my dad met his future father-in-law.

AFTER A FEW months of dating my mother, Dad got into a really bad car accident that sent him to a hospital in Toronto. He needed to get a skin graft. It was a serious accident that also required surgeons to replace nerves that were ripped off his spinal cord. It was a scary time in my dad's life. While there, he caught some Christian television programming where a little girl gave her testimony. Dad got down on his knees and prayed. This was the moment he accepted Jesus Christ as his saviour. He came back a changed man and told my mom that if they were to stay together, they were going to get married. They got married. They sobered up. They went to church every Sunday.

When they began to have children, my mother prayed to the same God she had prayed to as a child. This time her prayers were specific.

Please protect my children from any abuse.

Please, not my children.

Not them.

ten

EVEN THOUGH MOM COULDN'T PROTECT US EVERY minute of our childhood, I know that she tried. She cherished us and loved us the best she knew how.

She made sure I looked like a doll every day of kindergarten. I was a very well-dressed five-year-old with a perpetual perm.

Sometimes when Mom dropped me off at school, I would walk the long way around the brown brick building and make my way toward the far door. It was to avoid the Grade 7 students. I wanted to avoid them not because they were mean to me, but because they adored me. I was a shy kid. I couldn't have that kind of love thrown at me without very real introvert pain. Mom, with all of her good intentions in dressing me, had created me a fan club. And it brought attention that I didn't appreciate. The girls in

Grade 7 would circle around me in the mornings, their tall frames blocking my escape.

"Twirl again," they would say. Their fingers would reach down to pinch a cheek or trace over my mother's latest hair accessory.

Schoolyard objectification was difficult.

We went to church every Sunday and I remember running down the corridor of the Friendship Centre. That's where they held the Native Christian services in Dawson Creek. The people sang songs in Cree, a language I couldn't understand. Mom said that one time I was running around with the kids and stopped mid-stride. I got down on my knees to say a quick prayer then began to run around again. I was raised with the knowledge that God is everywhere.

Everywhere, even in the big brown house we lived in, which we got through Native housing. God was there too. I imagine Jesus sat out on that big deck with the scratchy green fake grass plastered on the floor. I bet it tickled his toes like it did mine. The house also served as a sanctuary for injured birds, which, in turn, attracted random and feral felines. They weren't the nice type of felines that purred and rubbed themselves against you. They were the asshole kind who had to have tenacity to survive, and they hissed at the sight of you. They were always showing up in the house, staking their claim. I learned that not all of God's creatures understand the concept of territory. I had many encounters with the colonial cats.

God was everywhere, but I learned that sometimes we had to be a reflection of God's love in the world.

One time, my dad took my brothers and me to the movie theatre. We sat down in a row, with our soda and popcorn in hand, ready for the movie to start. We were excited—that is, until my dad noticed three other little Native kids running around the theatre looking for discarded popcorn bags. They were hungry. My dad called those kids over. He removed our popcorn from our laps and gave it to the three children.

Dad says that he asked us if he could give it to them, but I remember being sad that my lap was suddenly empty. Our popcorn bags floated away from us in the hands of three happy little bobbing heads. I learned that we are a family that gives from what little we have.

Dad would read me stories at night. He told me years later that he had to force himself to read stories to us until he actually enjoyed reading to us. He said that he wasn't raised with bedtime stories. But he knew other parents read to their kids, so he did it too.

My dad broke a link in the chain of intergenerational dysfunction—one Dr. Seuss book at a time.

I loved listening to the stories. And it could very well be because of my dad's effort that I became a storyteller. It didn't matter that I was only in Grade 1 at the time. It started with the school assignment of journal writing. In my journal, I would write the most elaborate stories and share them with the other children at school. These were stories that featured my amazing pet unicorn, Sparkle, and my late pet chicken. Who tragically died in a barnyard fire. My pet chicken was the ultimate pet chicken. She was a character, let me tell ya.

Sparky the chicken did not just die an ordinary death. She died while saving all the other barnyard animals that lived on the imaginary farm that we most definitely did not live on. I would tell these stories, in colourful detail and with conviction. The other children would laugh and get excited about the world that I had created.

It landed me in trouble. My teacher called my mom, infuriated with my unwillingness to follow Grade 1 journal procedures.

"Helen needs to stop lying," she said. "She has all the other kids believing this nonsense and tells them these tall tales. Journal entries are for things that really happen in her everyday life, not for her to make up stuff."

I couldn't tell the truth about what was happening in my real life so I made shit up and used my imagination to create another world. I wouldn't say that I was lying. I was just a kid trying to survive her own reality by making up an alternate one. Imagination was my coping mechanism. It was a blanket I could pull over me to forget that I was being sexually abused.

How was I supposed to write a journal about how some man had made me watch him ejaculate while I was trying to eat my cereal? My stomach churned at the sight of cereal for an entire school year after that happened. I preferred Sparkle the Unicorn stories over talking about being forced to look at pornography and having some male interloper force himself on me. Joanne got to write about family trips and normal things like hopscotch in her journals. I didn't know what to write. Sparky the chicken didn't exist, but I bet that if she did, Sparky would have saved me.

No one really knew. I don't know how they didn't know that all of this was happening, but they didn't. I was so convinced that I was to blame, and because of that, I remained silent. I stopped writing about imaginary lives and wrote about what good moments I could find. It just meant that I had to look a little harder.

But, it wasn't just writing that helped me. Reading did the same. I became an avid reader at a very young age. Mom enrolled me in a summer reading program and would sign out a stack of books for me. I would devour them in one sitting and would be pulling on the hem of my mom's shirt the next day, demanding to be taken to the library. Mom would oblige, and we would go back for another stack of books. Finally, after days spent walking her three children to the library and back, mom had to sit me down and break it to me: "My girl, you just can't read so fast. We can't go to the library every day. You're going to have to wait a few days in between because I can't keep up."

I sat in my small fuzzy pink chair and lingered over the letters. I disappeared into books. Kids would knock on the door, asking, "Can Helen come out and play?"

I would holler back from my chair, "I can't play, I'm reading!"

But when I did get out to play, I would run over to my neighbour's house. They had a daughter. It was the best because our playtime included doing jump kicks off the coffee table. We would throw MC Hammer on the stereo and make up dance routines. Sometimes the teenage neighbour would let us come over. He taught us what he knew about basketball. That summer, I learned how to spin a basketball on my hand. But really, I only acted interested because he was a teenager. And he didn't have cooties. As a matter of fact, I thought the basketball-spinning neighbour was really cute.

Eventually we moved from our little town to Fort St. John and I achieved some level of normalcy. We had moved away from the abusers. I was free to be a child. I entered into the third grade with Coke-bottle glasses and very, very short brown hair that had been permed. My mother was big on perms all throughout elementary school. I walked through the doorway of that elementary school with my knees knocking. I had made it to the boot room when a young boy my age approached me.

"Hey buddy," he said.

"Yeah?" I answered sheepishly.

"My name is Ricky and anything you need, man, I'm here for ya," he told me with a solid pat on the back.

I didn't know what had happened there but I'm pretty sure I started off my first day of third grade as a boy. It continued. On the second day, a girl I had made friends with told me that she had said to her mom she met this really cool person named Helen but was unsure if "it" was a girl or boy. Her mother said I was probably a girl.

"So," she asked me, "are you a girl?"

I nodded and nibbled on my cheese sandwich while I vowed never to allow my mother to perm my hair again.

Months later, I went to a George Jones concert with my aunties. I was excited—it was my first real concert. I didn't really know the words but I danced and swayed in my seat and clapped my hands when I heard "I don't need your rockin' chair" come blaring from the speakers. After the concert was over, one of my aunties asked if we wanted to meet the band.

"Yes," I squealed.

We waited for most of the crowd to trickle out before we walked down the cement steps. Halfway down the steps my auntie stopped the drummer of the band.

"We loved the show," my auntie gushed.

"And what about you?" he turned to me and asked.

"I loved it too!" I said happily.

"That's great to hear, son!" he replied.

I started to cry instantly.

"What did I say?" he asked, puzzled.

"She's a girl," my auntie said as she pulled me toward her.

After my hair grew out, we moved across town and I went to a new school. I made new friends who knew I was a girl.

In class, I wrote a speech on how amazingly fun and rich reading is. To my terror, I was asked to recite it in front of the entire school. It would be good for me, they said. You can do anything you set your mind to, they said. I stood at the front of the gym, my paper shaking in my hand and beads of sweat forming on my nose. I thought to myself,

Damn it, Helen! Couldn't you have picked a cooler topic than reading?! I fumbled over words and tripped up over the part where I said reading could take you rafting. Reading can take you rafting?! I cursed myself again. Really cool, Helen. Really cool. From then on, public speaking became my number one enemy.

Despite my phobia of speaking in public, I still loved to read. And yes, it can take you rafting. Reading can transport you to another reality. Reading was a big part of my life. I would choose books over playtime outside any day of the week. I was never any good at sports and so I stuck to what I knew and what I loved. As a matter of fact, I tried to play baseball in the seventh grade and I lost our championship game because of my lack of athletic ability. The ball flew so slowly toward me that I could see it clearly against the sky of blue. I closed my eyes tightly, raised my mitt in the air, and heard a thud behind me. It was the thud that ended all my sports endeavours. My teammates avoided me after that. I felt like I was the kid with a chronic peeing problem. It was traumatic.

At the end of Grade 7, I had received straight As and my dad promised me that I could either (a) receive one thousand dollars or (b) do something of my choice that was close to an equivalent. I think I surprised the shit out of both of my parents when I chose option B. And that option was me going skydiving.

"She's only twelve years old, Richard!" my mom shrieked.

"I promised her . . ." my father replied calmly.

"Something else, anything else. Not my baby, not way up there," she pleaded.

"Shirley," my father said to her, "now I went and promised her that she could do anything she wanted if she brought home straight As. She's done that. I have to hold up my end of the bargain."

That was the end of the discussion. It just so happened that I had never been in a plane before and had a minor phobia of heights. It turned out that the minor phobia was actually a major phobia. Before I knew it, I was fastened tandem-style to my instructor at ten thousand feet in the air and found myself short of breath and experiencing temporary paralysis.

"Can I just go back down? . . . I mean I—I would rather have the money. Or you can just keep the money. Keep it. Keep it all," I stammered, my eyes pleading with my instructor.

I was sure that I had made a huge mistake. I would not survive this. I could see the aftermath of it all. *We are gathered here to mourn the loss of our brave adventurer Helen. She died flying like a free bird, and now she is truly free.* My mother would sob, perhaps she would punch my father in the face. The Bigfoot women can be unpredictable. They would all shake their solemn heads. *Taken so soon*, the crowd would murmur. *Straight-A student.* Sigh. *She showed such promise.*

My instructor paid me no mind. Instead, he laughed in my trembling face. "You can go down, all right," he yelled back at me, "but only by jumping out."

And away we went. I fell ten thousand feet, but I didn't know that was only the beginning of my descent. Later that year, I made the transition from elementary school to junior high. It was a fall from whatever bit of grace I had managed to scrape together.

It's been said to me so often that children don't see skin colour. That we are not born with the hatred of racism. It is something we are taught. I believe this. Adolescence taught me this.

I MET AMANDA in Grade 6. Amanda. We would walk home every day together. In the harsh northern winters, we would tug on our snow pants and pull on our mitts and begin the cheek-biting trek. It wasn't that far, maybe four or five blocks, but in −30°C it feels like a marathon. A marathon with frozen goods slapping your face the entire way, with tear ducts and a nose that drip for no apparent reason.

Amanda came to my house for sleepovers. She ate at my kitchen table. I played at her house, I cuddled her ugly Shih Tzu dog. We did homework assignments together. We were pretty close to being best friends. My father had nicknames for her, but my father had nicknames for everyone. I think this is because it serves his memory to name people things like "Marshmallow" or "Miatz" ("ugly" in Cree). When I got straight As in Grade 7 and chose to go skydiving, my father allowed me to take a friend. Guess who got to go with me?

Amanda.

Sure enough, we entered the war zone of junior high together. But Amanda and I were lucky enough to have a social studies class together too. We sat side by side whenever we could. If one got to class before the other, an item would be placed on the desk next to her to make it appear as if it was occupied. We were tight like that.

In social studies, we were learning about the Treaty-making process in the Midwest. At the time, we were learning about the Cree. The textbook we were learning from said that a specific tribe of Cree was offered so many acres of land for each family. The Cree turned down the offer and were upset. The Cree demanded more land.

For me, this was supposed to be a time where I could learn about my history too. It was as if I was reading about my great-great-grandfathers and grandmothers. I was excited. Then, to my utter and complete horror, I heard Amanda say angrily, "Greedy bastards. I wouldn't have gave them any land."

I wanted to slam the textbook shut. I wanted to ball my little mixed-blood fists up and pummel them into her porcelain cheeks. I wanted to pull out a few strands of her blonde hair. I wanted to gouge the blue right out of her eyes. I wanted to tell her to shut up. I wanted to yell at the teacher and tell him there's got to be more to the story.

I did none of these things. I felt my face turn red with shame. I fidgeted in my seat. I felt betrayed and upset and hurt. I wanted to scream. This was the first time (of many more to come) in my life that I really and truly feel as if I was categorized as "the other."

I became "the other" in my eighth-grade social studies class. The outcast.

The wild Indian.

Merciless Indian savage.

The living, breathing, walking, heaving stereotype.

This is the year I start drinking and smoking pot.

Everyone says pot isn't a gateway drug, and I would believe that too, if it wasn't for my own stupid-ass decisions.

I was visiting Her. *The* Her, and she had a pile of cocaine sitting on her end table. We were thirteen years old. "Do you want to try it?" she asked.

I shifted on her bed, interested, but I knew nothing about cocaine.

"Nah, but I'll blaze," I answered as I reached for the pop can we'd washed out earlier.

I began to make a pipe out of the pop can for the baggie of roaches we had collected that week. As I made the pipe she cut up the roaches, sticky papers and all. We smoked our roaches and she added another small chunk of bud that wasn't enough for a joint on top of the holes. We were joking around when she stopped and started cutting up lines of cocaine. I watched her, stoned and fascinated. I was high as fuck and doing cocaine looked kind of cool now.

"I wanna try!" I squealed as I bounced myself sitting on the edge of her bed.

"Okay! Come here and sit down. I'll make you a small one."

I kneeled on the floor beside her as she made a sliver of a line and passed me the cut straw. I snorted that one. She snorted one. I snorted another. She snorted another. We shared the last line.

We heard a honk outside.

"Shit, it's my dad!" I laughed, high and displaced. "I gotta go."

"Helen, wait!" she said as I reached for the handle.

"What?"

"You got powder under your nose!" she said, laughing.

I giggled and wiped the coke from my thirteen-year-old nose and walked out into the darkness.

The story spirals from there.

I lost my virginity. I slept with another guy. I don't remember any of this but heard about it when I was sober. I began to hate myself immensely. I didn't know how to control myself, and the girl in me that was sexually abused for so long surfaced. "Remember me?" she said. She came to fuck shit up until she was listened to. I did not listen. Instead, I tried to silence her with more blow, more booze. She would not be pacified. She reached for other people's skin when I was drunk. I lost my grip on my controls and she became the kamikaze pilot intent on killing us both.

Partway through the school year is when I was brutally raped and left on the outskirts of town. That is when I moved to Prince George for the first time. When Mom had to hold my hand as I lay on the examination table while a rape kit was being done. I couldn't stay in Fort St. John after that attack. I felt like a pariah once news about the rape became known. I became the subject of everyone's whisper campaign.

I got beat up by a nineteen-year-old before I left that town. Someone got questioned about my rape and their cousin was not having that. I moved with a busted lip and a bruised cheek. I learned it's better to keep your mouth shut no matter what. I packed my bags and my dad drove me to Prince George to live with my auntie on my dad's side. I was not very close with my dad's family, but she took me in.

Day one at that new high school made me realize that no matter where I moved, my problems moved with me. It offered little comfort that the student population was three times larger than at the last school I attended. I suppose I should have thought about that factor in terms of how it could be easier to blend in. Instead, I could only foresee three times the ridicule. I knew I'd probably fuck up again.

It was completely bizarre going to school and discovering that hardly anyone was Native. I met all the Native people on the first day. There was a core group that I hung out with and we would blaze together during our lunch breaks. One night the boys got their hands on some acid and we dropped that and took turns sliding down an icy slanted driveway on our asses. Two of the guys decided to get in a "friendly fist fight" and, not wanting to see it, I went back inside and ended up locking myself in the bathroom to stare at my face.

Your face doesn't look like your face while you're on drugs.

The mirror feels like a portal to an alternate universe, one where you see you are wearing an alien's skin and parading around as if it is your own. The eyes seem familiar but the rest of it is foreign. I moved the skin on my cheeks around to make sure it was my face, my skin, my body. I stared at the alien for thirty minutes before I unlocked the door. I went back out into the madness. I was drawn to it.

I finally saw a familiar face at school, an anchor to home. I saw her (*the* Her) sister at the school. She had moved to Prince George as well and I told her if she needed anything I was there for her. I would do what any sister would do and protect her. Even though we weren't friends then, it was comforting to have her there.

The feeling was short-lived. A week later, we were sitting in math class when the small, cute blonde that the sister had been hanging around turned to me and asked, "So why did you move from Fort St. John?"

"I just did," I answered flatly.

"I heard it's because you were a slut and got raped."

I could barely swallow the ball that formed in my throat.

"That is a fucking lie," I replied angrily.

When the bell rang, I walked into the hallway, my whole body vibrating. I couldn't have it follow me to this new place. The stories. The stares. I wanted to vomit. I saw the sister walking down the hallway and I walked up to her. I shoved her into a locker.

"Get the fuck outside," I growled.

"Leave me alone," she bit back and made a beeline for the entrance.

"I'm going to kick your fucking teeth in," I barked from behind.

As we neared the entrance, she spoke quickly to the guy who was her boyfriend at the time. He grabbed on to me. Hard.

"Get the fuck off me!" I yelled as I watched her head toward the front door.

I managed to wriggle loose and ran behind her. I shoved her again. Her face slammed into the push handle of the door. The boyfriend grabbed me again and I watched her walk outside and away from me. I couldn't escape the stories. I got suspended the next day for smoking pot. I got kicked out of my auntie's that weekend for drinking. I was back in self-destruct mode.

I learned that the world is unkind to "sluts who get raped."

After all, sluts can't get raped. Sluts get told in so many ways that rape is inevitable. The words *slut* and *rape* used in the same sentence have the effect of cancelling each other out. Or rather, they cancel out the validity of the rape because people still point to the sluttery as a reason why the slut got raped.

If I was a different kind of girl with a different kind of story, and a different kind of heritage, maybe all the messages would have all been different. Maybe I would have just been a girl who got raped, which is hard enough on its own. But at least I would have been allowed some space to feel somewhat outraged about the act of being raped.

Dad came to Prince George to pick me up. I enrolled back in the same junior high in the new school year. Some time had passed. And everyone knows that the passage of time allows for healing. Or forgetting. I found when I did return that the rumours had settled—making it easier for me to settle in as well.

My first class back at my old school was gym. I was feeling sweaty—and tired in so many ways—so I asked the principal, "What time is that break?"

We stood beside each other in the gymnasium.

"I'm not sure exactly, 10:15?" he replied.

"No . . . I think it's 10:25. I am pretty sure it got shifted."

"You know? I think you're right," he said.

"Pretty sure you should make me vice principal," I said as I bumped my elbow into his.

"Sure."

"What?"

"Let's make you vice principal for the day," he said, smiling.

"All right!" I exclaimed.

I was vice principal for an entire day the following week. I got to sit in on boring meetings and stroll the hallway and kick kids back into their classes.

"Get to class."

"I don't have to listen to you," a kid would spit back.

"I'm the fuckin' vice principal today, didn't you hear? Get your ass back to class before I take you to the office."

Power didn't sit well with me. Lending truth to the saying, Be fearful when the oppressed become the oppressors.

My time as a respected administrator was short-lived. Five months later, my friends and I got caught with flasks taped to our legs as we were trying to get into the year-end dance. The principal sat across from me in his office, "Now Helen, I know that you are an honest girl. Did you guys drink earlier tonight too?"

I was drunk in his chair trying to think of a reply. Nothing came.

"Helen, were you guys drinking before you came?"

"I—I . . . I'm drunk."

I get slapped with a suspension and my vice principal days were left behind me.

That year, I got a summer job at the Friendship Centre. I was hired as a receptionist. I was the family fuck-up but for that summer I tried to hold my shit together. I had to step up. It's because my mom was still drinking at that point and was falling apart more and more. I did all the grocery shopping and the laundry and tried to have hot meals on the table for my brothers and Dad.

No one remembers this summer I was the woman of the house. No one.

My grandma (Dad's biological mom) visited that summer, which was a rare occurrence and still is a very rare occurrence indeed. I was downstairs watching the television when she came and sat beside me. Dad's family has never shown signs of affection. We didn't even hug.

That day, Grandma placed her brown hand on my lap and left it there. I became very aware that this was an even odder occurrence than her presence in our home. I squirmed beneath her hand and finally moved over on the couch, leaving her hand grasping nothing but seat. Grandma waited a minute before she moved herself closer toward me. She placed her hand on my leg again. I sat for a few seconds longer before I moved farther down the couch. I became hyper-aware of her presence beside me and finally it got so awkward that I had to get up and walk away.

It wasn't until years later that I realized that Grandma was reclaiming the ability to show affection. My grandma's brown hand on my knee was the hand of resilience. Hers were hands that were learning how to love again.

Later that year I was at a bonfire party out of town. I was standing with a boy who was visiting from a nearby reservation when a group of drunken cowboys surrounded us.

"Is this here your squaw?" one of the cowboys asked him.

The cowboys all began to jeer and laugh. The boy stood silent. His eyes burned a hole into the mud beneath our feet.

"Looks like a squaw to me," the chubby cowboy said as he grabbed at me.

I hit his hand away and I swore at them and they laughed harder. My girlfriend had gotten punched in the face by cowboys at a bush party. Racism and violence didn't include the acknowledgement of gender differences.

They made obscene comments and grabbed themselves and grabbed at me while calling me names. The boy I was with had lost his voice. Finally the cowboys tired and walked away laughing into the darkness while the boy stood still looking at the ground. With my face still flushed and stinging with shame I walked past him and knocked the beer out of his hand.

"Bastard," I said.

I started to hate Native men that night. I hated myself and I hated the addiction that crippled me, my mother, my family, and the Natives I saw on the street. I hated that being a Native girl made me feel like I was disposable and that it gave white boys the right to grab at me whenever they wanted. I hated the skin that I belonged in and the people I belonged to. I didn't want to belong to them.

I didn't know the stories of where we came from as a people. Those stories had been taken out of the mouths of my mother, of my father, who grew up disconnected from everything that made us strong as a people. I didn't know that my great-great-grandfather had signed the Treaty or that I came from a bloodline of resistance and strength. All I saw was weakness.

I was in the dreamless void.

Part Three
The Healing

eleven

IT IS AMAZING TO ME HOW FAR A LITTLE CLARITY can take you.

A month after the peyote ceremony outside of Edmonton I checked myself in to a treatment centre.

Peyote had cleared the pathway. I still needed to make the journey.

There was work to be done.

Trauma needed to be unknotted.

Memories needed to be cleansed.

I needed to set myself free.

MY HANDS TREMBLED when I walked into her office. The counsellor assigned to me at the treatment centre was an older lady with a no-nonsense attitude about her. She was strict, and her serious tone and authoritative demeanour scared me. After our second meeting I realized she wasn't so scary, she just knew out to snap addicts out of their behaviours. I sat in a wood-framed chair with faded tan cushions. I cradled my knees and stared off into the corner of the room. There were pictures and paintings of buffalo and warriors on the wall. Sunlight streamed in through the windows that framed the manicured bushes on the grounds outside. Medicine was laid out on one of her shelves. A hooped braid of sweetgrass and a bundle of sage were ready to witness and cleanse those who entered the room. I was safe. I knew that to find true healing I would have to venture further than I had ever gone before. I'd need to spill out all my skeletons. I would need to pick the bones of buried secrets from my throat to make it easier for me to breathe.

I needed to tell the cutting story.

I needed to talk about those men hurting me and how it made me feel.

As I spoke, my words trembled. They were so unsure of coming out into the world. The story clung to my throat. It did not want to see the light of day. I pulled it out of me. Dragged it out of me. It was painful. My body forced itself into the fetal position in the wooden chair. I rocked myself, gasping slightly for air.

The skeletons tried to choke out the light. I talked about the blood on my hands. The flesh that was cut. Flesh of my flesh. Blood of my blood.

A story. Words. Words attached to trauma. Trauma tied my body to memory. The body remembers.

I cried in the chair. Hands over knees. Rocking myself as if I were my own baby. Hush now.

My counsellor grabbed both of my arms and looked me straight in the eyes.

"Helen," she said. "Helen, look at me."

I stared at the corner of the room.

"Helen," she repeated. "You need to know that it was not your fault. It's not your fault. No one, and I mean no one, has the right to harm you. You have the right to be safe from harm at all times."

"But . . . ," I whispered, "I was drinking."

"No, it doesn't matter if you were drunk or high or sober or whatever. Your body is your own and no man or woman has a right to violate you or harm you. You hear me?"

I couldn't look her in the eyes.

"Do you hear me, Helen? It's not your fault. I want to hear you say it."

"It's not my fault," I said. An avalanche of tears escaped down my face. "It's not my fault," I repeated again a little louder.

My mouth pushed out the words but I didn't believe them.

"Put your feet flat on the floor," she instructed. "Keep yourself grounded, Now breathe. Take deep breaths."

My counsellor referred me to the treatment centre's psychologist who visited twice a week.

A FEW DAYS later I sat in the psychologist's office. She was an elderly white lady with short hair who didn't look like she could navigate morally shocking conversations with ease. She did. She never batted an eyelash when I told her about the men who cut me.

"Let me draw one for you so you can show me where the damage is," she said softly as she placed a Post-it on her desk.

I was twenty-four years old and I did not yet know the correct names for the parts of my own vagina. I felt like a curious child, waiting to see a mythical creature be revealed. I sat in the chair, half petrified because I knew that in order for any of this to work I had to be honest.

"And this right here is your labia," she indicated with a pencil point and then continued to sketch out the nooks and crannies. Her voice was soothing and hypnotic. Immediately, my discomfort disappeared. My racing heartbeat lowered. I had never been sat down like this and shown such naked, raw care.

"Now doesn't that just look like a tulip?" she asked, looking at the picture in silent awe.

I showed her where the cuts had occurred and where a bulb of flesh still hung on. I felt like shrinking back into my seat but the look in her eyes and the trusting smile on her face coaxed me forward.

"Do you want to see a gynecologist, dear?"

I nodded.

Her voice continued to flow in a melodic manner and I felt like I was in a dream. She singsonged her way through the alphabet of the phone book. Her lips let out an "Aha" upon finding the phone number to the clinic. "There is always a terribly long wait, but you just watch me work my magic!" she said to me.

By the end of the phone call, I was booked to see the gynecologist the following week. Tears of gratitude made their way home on my lap. I had never treated myself with such gentleness, love, and care. I had never believed that I deserved that level of love and care before. It was the first time I realized that maybe I wasn't a social and sexual leper, that maybe—just maybe—I was worthy of loving myself. I'm not sure the psychologist herself realized the magnitude of healing that came from that afternoon of Post-its and a phone call.

I struggled deeply with this concept of "not my fault." It's true that I believed the guilt and shame of rape should not be relegated to those whose bodies are violated. I believed this so much. I had even talked about it publicly. It was a few months earlier, before I sobered up. I was trying so hard to convince myself that it was never my fault.

Somewhere I'd found the courage to stand in front of a jam-packed coffee house on International Women's Day. I spoke about women being the givers of life. I said that our bodies are sacred. A traditional teaching. I spoke about how an attack on a woman is more than just an attack on the physical body. I spoke about how that type of physical violence also damages the spirit. I talked about how that damage is never isolated just to the victim. It ripples out, potentially destroying a family, a social circle, even a whole community.

I read the following poems:

(PART ONE)
You can keep your sex
it's what you risked it all for.

Forgot your humanness,
forgot my humanness.
We both disappeared
into the angry void of your lust.

It's what you wanted,
what you came for,
but it's the least of
what you took.

You can keep your sex.

You can keep
your grunting and groaning,
skins colliding with thunderclaps,
sounds like more
than just bodies breaking
to me.

You can keep your
desensitized sweat beads,
they trickle down
and stain me,
stinging flesh
like unprovoked bees.
Welts invisible
they form inside me.

You can keep
your angry buttocks
beating into chasms
that may never
be full again.

You can keep
your one-sided ecstasy,
sweet releases.

Moments you
fought for
hurt for
killed for.

You can keep your
badly coloured dreams
that penetrate
parts of me
I thought out of reach.

You can keep your sex,
but I will keep me.

(PART TWO)
No more time lapses,
and moments stalled in recollection.
No more recycling of
apprehended seconds.

No more trying to scrub clean
where soap just can't reach.
No more sleepless nights,
and post traumatic dreams.

No more pointing
fingers back at ourselves.
No more playbacks of
how it felt.
No more donning loose clothing
and dimmed-down smiles.

No more feeling like bodies
are mere spaces waiting to be defiled.
No more being afraid to be yourself
and attract the wrong attention.
No more given over to
these ill intentions . . .

No more girls.
Women.
No more spreading of stubborn legs,
and breaking of brave hearts.
No more smashing of strong souls,
or torches or trauma being passed on.
No more telling little girls to be strong,
and being raped by men we know.
No more having to say that no means no,
and taking it lightly or turning a blind eye.
No more vaginal reconstructions and bruised thighs.
No more unsafe streets and take back the nights.
No more sisters and spirit vigils.
No more fighting for what is our birthright.
No more double standards for different countries.
No more silencing of victims and
    shunning of survivors.

No more acting like it hasn't happened,
doesn't happen,
isn't happening now,
to the women that we know.

Our friends.
Our sisters.
Our daughters.
Our mothers.
Ourselves.

No more words.
Just Change.
But until there is no more,
there are still words left to say.

Women cried after I read my poems. Strangers hugged me afterwards. People were proud that I had the courage to speak my truth.

I thought about that moment many times over the next five weeks at the treatment centre. But was I brave speaking out as I did? It was only an illusion of bravery.

I tried to convince myself that I had dealt fearlessly with the traumatic events that marred my past. The truth was that I had never allowed myself to feel the emotions surrounding the sexual abuse and rapes that I'd endured. Under all of the bravado I was a lost little Indian girl, secretly afraid that I was the source of all the trouble. It was the secret I wanted to take to the grave. Afraid that if I ever uttered it, someone would confirm my suspicion: *It is all your fault, Helen.*

This was my great hypocrisy, my disconnection between truth and thought. In order to heal my warrior spirit, I would have to face the lies I told myself. I had been convincing myself of these lies for two decades. They fit on me like truths. They were a little uncomfortable and they rubbed me the wrong way but they were the only things that I knew.

The real truth is that I am a war-worthy woman and deserving of respect. But it was something I'd need to learn.

AS PART OF treatment, my visits to the psychologist became routine. She encouraged me to cry. I was reading a book by Terry Tempest Williams. *When Women Were Birds.* Williams says that a woman is being her true authentic self when she cries. For the next few days after speaking openly to the psychologist, I was the most authentic I had been in a long damned time.

My hardline-drawing counsellor was much different than the singsongy, soft psychologist. I was in her office and began talking about different affirmations I was using. I wanted to show her I was capable of making change. I talked about some self-help strategies from books that I was going to start using. Visualization. Manifestation.

"Helen," she said, her voice telling me I was on the wrong track.

"Yes?"

"You realize you are a client, right? You have some training in social work but you are not here to fix yourself with what you know. You have to let yourself be a client."

I wasn't sure exactly what she meant and didn't know what to say.

"I notice you are analytical and think things through. You are always trying to mentally navigate yourself toward a better place or fix things. You spend a lot of time in your head. You need to focus on your emotions and spiritual aspects too."

I nodded. I began to follow her thoughts but still couldn't grasp exactly what she was trying to tell me. She looked exasperated because I wasn't following her thoughts.

"I'm banning you from books. How many did you bring anyways?"

"What?!" I croaked out, stunned by the sheer ludicrousness of it.

"No books, unless it's on a weekend. Now, how many did you bring?"

"Four."

"Great, let's write a contract. You can sign it and then give your books to the client worker to lock up."

I didn't have a choice. I think I am one of the only people in rehab history who has been banned from self-help material. Reading and writing has always been my sturdy crutch through thick and thin. It offers release. It offers escape. There is something stable in unshifting ink on paper.

But the counsellor wouldn't let me escape anymore. It was time to get real.

I REMEMBER WHEN my love affair with reading intensified.

I was in Grade 4. We had just moved into a bluish-grey townhouse complex. It sat across from the elementary school where I'd be attending. It was in this school, while donning short frizzy permed hair and Coke-bottle glasses, that I discovered William Shakespeare. I actually aspired to become William Shakespeare until I found out that I couldn't transform into a dead old white dude. I was sorely disappointed. I had a permanent loan on an old copy of his collected works.

I was not your average kid in the fourth grade. I devoured *Macbeth*, lived and breathed *Romeo and Juliet*, and had dreams about *Hamlet*. My father, wanting to encourage me in my affinity for the arts, took me on a father-daughter date to a theatrical performance of *The Taming of the Shrew*. I sat at the edge of my seat, engulfed in a northern town's low-budget re-enactment of my idol's work.

I fell deeply in love with words, with their positioning and the on-paper dance that they orchestrate. I began to write poetry about knights in shining armour. I wrote about being rescued from the humdrum of my daily life. I even wrote a poem entitled "Mister President." I forced my family to sit down in a horseshoe-shaped fashion to listen to me recite. No one—I repeat, no one in my family—took me aside to tell me that we live in Canada. We do not have a president. We have a prime minister.

To this day, I still insist on reciting my poetry to my family. I often call my dad at random—day or night—and insist that he listen to one of my poems. He laughs when I do this, "All right, my girl." Maybe it reminds him of when I was in Grade 4. But he always lends an ear.

I spent hours as a kid consulting my dictionary and would tuck away words in my mind that I heard adults use to look up later. I was that annoying kid who followed my cousins around saying, "Ask me to spell something. Go on, ask me." I was relentless. "G-Y-M-N-A-S-I-U-M. Gymnasium. Ask me another one. Go on, ask me."

I worked hard at memorizing passages of *Romeo and Juliet*. Not to recite to anyone in particular. It was more or less to impress myself. Shakespeare would have *so* been impressed, I would think to myself, after reciting in my mirror. I became a hopeless romantic at an early age.

We went to church every Sunday. As we sat in the pew, I dutifully read from the pretty little white leather Bible that my mother had given me. It had a little silver lamb with poofy hair on the front that I thought was adorable. I set out on reading the entire Bible. I was, after all, a kid who wanted to impress Shakespeare, and I definitely wanted to get on the good side with this guy Jesus too.

I had no idea that what was written in that Bible would upset me to the point of not being able to function. That happened one quiet afternoon. I was visiting with my auntie and reading a part of the Old Testament. The passage talked about sexual deviation and sexual offences. It promised that those acts would be punished by hellfire and by being cast into the darkness and the grinding of teeth.

This couldn't be right, I thought to myself. I read it again.

How could I go to hell? I went to church every Sunday. I was a smart girl who listened to her parents and sang all the gospel songs. I prayed at every meal. All I could think about was all the sexual stuff that cluttered up my childhood.

And what I read in the Old Testament caused me to panic. I was looking at eternal damnation.

Penises. Tongues. Fingers. Secrets.

I dropped my Bible on my bedroom floor and began to cry. I couldn't breathe. I was breathing too much. I didn't know what was happening. All of the *TeenBeat* magazine pull-out posters on my wall and crocheted doilies on my bedside table began to spin around me.

Nothing made sense and I couldn't get a grip on anything to make it stop spinning. I needed my world to become stable. I half ran, half stumbled down the stairwell. I fell to the floor at the bottom of the steps. I was crying so hard I couldn't even pick myself up.

I was going to hell. The Bible said so. I was a bad girl and I was going to be punished. It was all right there in ink on paper.

My auntie who lived with us rushed over to me and carried my small body to the couch. I continued sobbing and crying from a place of deep hurt. I remember crying in such a way only a handful of times. This was one of them.

A dozen times, my auntie tried to get me to tell her the reason behind my Grade 4 breakdown. I kept crying, my small body shaking like a lonely autumn leaf on a windy day clutching at life. I couldn't talk if I had wanted to and I couldn't tell her my secrets even if I could have talked. No one could know that I was such a bad girl. She held my head in her lap and stroked my hair until I finally fell asleep. My tiny body was still shuddering from the labour of my tears.

They were just words I read in the Bible. But they were words that condemned me.

There was one other formative time that I carried with me. Words are funny like that. Words were my everything as an avid reader and wannabe writer, but they also had the power to instill crippling beliefs that lasted decades. Years later I was running wild so my parents sent me away for a while, to stay with one of my aunties out at a ranch.

The aunties served as second mothers. Whenever I was in trouble and my parents didn't know what else to do, they shipped me off to an auntie. The aunties all had a similar process. They would allow me to get used to my environment. Then their auntie Spidey sense kicked in, and they knew when I'd reached the comfort zone. It was after that they would launch into "the talk." The talk was always a mix of advice, inquiry, and a stern scolding for not respecting my parents. So, there I was on the ranch in the middle of nowhere, waiting for the talk. I read all of Auntie's books in her immensely small library, which all dealt with clichéd romance, and when I wasn't reading I was doing manual labour.

My auntie and I were outside of her log cabin putting in a fence to keep out the buffalo that roamed free in the territory. I don't remember everything, but I do remember when she said, "Helen, one day you are going to fall in love. You will find an amazing man who is everything that you have ever wanted but you will have to tell this man every-thing that you have ever done. And chances are, he won't love you anymore."

The words were digested through my ears and made a home in my stomach. A knotted ball that would take years to be unravelled.

I was fifteen but had already slept with more men than I cared to count. I had been to a treatment centre—twice. I accepted that I would probably never be truly loved in a green valley of plenty and under a blue sky. I would never have the romance that the books I read depicted. I died a small death that day.

WITHOUT READING, MY mind ran buck wild. It visited moments like the one with my auntie. I guess that was the point of me getting banned from books. I had to remember the hard moments and challenge their validity to take up so much goddamned space in my head.

I didn't know how to function without reading or trying to think my way through things. But my books were gone. I was jonesing for a read. *Just. One. More. Line.* I've said that line before. I was forced to sit in the common area flipping through the encyclopedia. There was only the letter A. And it was the only book.

I learned about some shit that went down in Alabama. In November of 1833, an event occurred called the Night the

Stars Fell. This night was one of the largest recorded meteor showers ever. The "stars" fell for three nights and many people believed that it was the end of the world. Judgement Day would surely follow. So, many people started to make amends. Slavery was still very much present at that time. But, fearing the end was close, some people were set free. Others told people their family origins and histories. Old feuds were settled. For three nights, the people of Alabama stood still. They held their breath under a falling sky, awaiting the end. After that, people told stories by using the event as an identifier. Things happened either before the stars fell, or after the stars fell. Noting the passage of time like that was terribly romantic. I was love-drunk.

I sat at the table in the common room, dreamy eyed over a faded encyclopedia. There must have been a young man who loved a young woman but something separated them. Their stars were crossed. Maybe she came from money and he was poor. Perhaps her older brother picked on him when they were young boys and he finally snapped and gave him a lickin' he would neither forget nor forgive. Of course, in this imagined love story everyone was white. Anytime I transport myself back into time to entertain favourable romance, the characters are white. My everyday reality already included the complicated dynamics of race and oppression. I didn't need that meddling with my daydreaming and time travel.

On the first night, when murmurs broke the silence of awe and word trickled across the county that this might be the end, he would have run to check on her. On the second night, when the stars persisted, he would have taken her by the hand and they would have ran away together and made love with the falling stars as witnesses to their blossoming love. On the third night, with the belief that the world was going to end, they would have bared their souls to each other. Spilled their innards on the table beside the kerosene lamp and each wound would have been given the air it needed to heal. After that third night, it would be as if they had been together for all of their lives.

Without books I had to make up my own stories.

"What are you looking all happy about?" asked Lexie in her chirpy voice.

Lexie was a cocaine addict/alcoholic. Before she got hooked, she had graduated at the top of her class with a master's degree. Now, her reality included living just a step up from street-level using. Addiction doesn't give a fuck how smart you are.

"Ahh, nothing. Just daydreaming over this stupid encyclopedia. Might as well read the dictionary," I said as I closed the book.

"Oh, you know what would be fantastic?"

"What's that?"

"If we picked up a few new words for our vocabulary every day," she said excitedly.

I am equal part dork so I replied enthusiastically, "Can we start right now?"

"Yes! Let's," Lexie said as she sat beside me.

We committed to using the words we'd learn as part of everyday conversation. I was still that relentless child hell-bent on learning.

Our word games provided some comic relief in an otherwise serious setting. We would seek out words that weren't commonplace. Words you wouldn't catch being thrown around a rehab. Then we would use said words in conversation that day.

We were in the smoking area when Lexie waved her hand, dismissively yet gracefully, toward another client. She reminded me of some 1950s Hollywood starlet. Her small frame, wavy short black hair, pretty face. Daintily waving a cigarette, she said, "Oh Phillip, don't be such a curmudgeon."

"Cur-what?" Phillip said with a confused look on his face.

Lexie and I began to giggle. Soon enough we had two other addicts standing around every morning with us learning new words to throw around. We were a bunch of meth-heads and cocaine addicts talking pretentiously over morning coffee.

"Due to unforeseen and trying circumstances I had developed a strong chemical dependency. I was inclined to become obliterated at regular intervals."

Can't no one say addicts are illiterate now.

It was a way to fill up time. We had to learn again to be normal functioning people and do normal things. To deal with time on our hands. Or to not deal with time on our hands . . . because it's illegal.

Another game we loved was Scrabble. It became a very competitive nighttime activity. We sat around a table, sometimes in the cafeteria, sometimes out in the sun, and tried our best to form seven-letter words. Or even better, tried to make use of the triple-word score. It set off a heated argument once. Someone insisted on using slang.

"It's a fuckin' word! I don't care if it's not in that stupid fuckin' dictionary or not!"

"You can't just make shit up and call it English, bro."

When it was apparent the men were not going to back down and it could end with fists flying, one of the other guys piped in, "Shit, guys, I thought we were playing Scrabble, not Squabble!"

Everyone started laughing. The guys shook off their bulldog tendencies, smiled, and sat back down.

"Go ahead and play the word, bro."

"Nah, it's cool. I'll play by the book."

Humour diffuses everything. This is how board games are played in rehab.

I have another memory of Scrabble, but it's G-R-O-S-S. Triple-word score. I was playing with an older client. He was not all there after years of street-level using. It was his turn.

"R-A-P-E," he spelled out the word aloud as he plunked the tiles down, then affirmed it out loud: "Rape."

My gut twisted. I stopped breathing. After that, the game felt dirty. I grabbed my letters and silently laid down F-E-V-E-R. I excused myself from playing another round and walked back down the women's wing to my room. One of the other guys saw me leave. It was obvious I was upset. He walked over to check the board after I left.

Later, I was outside smoking and it must have bothered him enough for him to approach me to talk about it.

"Hey, uh, you okay?"

"Why wouldn't I be? I mean, I'm here, aren't I?" I said as I waved my arm around and let out a small bleak laugh.

"No, I mean I seen what Kevin put down on that board. After you walked away I went to check because I knew something was wrong. He spelled 'rape,' man. That's fucked up. You okay?"

I didn't know how to answer his question. So, I gave a glib response. "Well, it's okay. I'm over it now," I said.

"You should bring it up during self-care circle, man. That shit wasn't cool," he said seriously.

"I'll think about it," I said. I stubbed out my cigarette and walked back inside.

Self-care circle was a practice in setting boundaries. It was one of the most awkward things I have ever had to do. As grown-ass addicts with behaviours and dysfunctions, we were likely to overstep boundaries and rub each other the wrong way. Self-care circle was about learning how to address those things in a healthy way. We would sit in the room where all of our large-group work took place. All of us sat in circle formation in the sunken session area. A wooden fence-like structure encircled us, with one way in, one way out. The counsellors sat behind the circle and fence and observed us from their elevated perch during self-care circle.

Sometimes it felt like a twisted game show.

May the odds be ever in your favour.

The formula is basic. The client says, "I feel [insert feeling] when you, [name of person], do this [specific action]. I request that you respect my [insert feeling/emotion/etc.] by [insert remedy]."

The person named will usually respond and apologize. They are encouraged to respect the other person. Sometimes it would result in yelling matches, flying cuss words, and increased tensions. I saw a big man fling a chair into the middle of the circle once. I half expected some wrestling moves and finishers to follow. The counsellors would try to step in at these moments and talk the people through it before it got out of hand. Sometimes it was never in hand in the first place.

So there I was in circle, dry mouthed and squirming in my seat.

"I felt unsafe when you, Kevin, spelled the word *rape* when we played Scrabble together. I request that you don't use that word at all, not even in games," I said, shifting again before going silent.

"It was just a game," Kevin piped up angrily.

Silence.

One of the counsellors spoke up, "Kevin, she is saying she felt unsafe. The point of the matter is that words like that should not be used in this centre, period. You don't know what other people have been through or what will trigger them. It's a matter of respecting other people."

"Okay," Kevin said, "I won't use that word again. I'm sorry."

Deep breath of relief. Boundary setting starts somewhere, even if it is awkward. I had never learned how to set

boundaries in a healthy way. Living there, it was required—
otherwise there would have been fist fights and Lord knows
what else going on.

Stabbings for sure.

I joke. But seriously. A total possibility.

We all fell into the rhythm of life there. Each day was
a little different but always had some combination of the
same activites. Eat. Therapy. Group therapy. Eat. Sweat
Lodge. Chores. Alcoholics Anonymous. Gym. Therapy. Eat.

I went through the motions but struggled with the waves
that working through my trauma brought down on me. I
couldn't catch my breath. One afternoon my emotions were
rubbed raw after an intense session with the psychologist.
It was lunchtime. I stood in line, not wanting to eat. But
if I didn't eat I wouldn't have a meal till dinnertime so I
grabbed a salad and quietly seated myself at one of the several
wooden circular dining tables next to three other clients. I
took a bite of my salad, grating the leaves between my teeth
rigidly, barely able to open my throat enough to swallow. I
sat at the table still rattled.

Half-present.

"Hey Jake, chew with your goddamn mouth closed, will
ya?" Mark said from across the table, nodding toward the
chickpeas and lettuce mingling visibly in his mouth.

Jake, a devoted member of the big-boys-die-hard club,
stuck his tongue out to display his food to everyone.

"Damn it, now if you only avoided whisky like you do yer table manners . . . then you wouldn't be in this mess, and I wouldn't have to stare at your face every fuckin' meal."

Laughter erupted, and I managed to laugh, but mid-chuckle I began to cry. It was that awkward cry where a laugh slowly morphs into a sob. It is like watching an accident happen in slow motion. You want to stop it. You see it coming. But there is nothing you can do. My lunch companions looked toward their food and examined their plates politely as my emotions hijacked my body and I started to sob.

It was a normal occurrence there. Unpredictable weeping at inopportune moments. It's an act that no one brings up after the fact but you still feel like the emotional leper in the moment. Emotions fuck with addicts. They can be the equivalent of cyanide to skin. We have learned to survive and survival didn't require emotions, it required that they were absent.

I rose from the table quickly and scurried to my room at the end of the women's wing, where I continued to cry.

I was not used to allowing myself feelings for my own pain. Crying without becoming severely angry with myself for doing so was hard. Tears that came whenever they pleased irritated me. So there I was, shaking from crying so hard, swearing into my pillow and kicking my feet like a child having a fit.

Clenched fist. Mattress. Open hand. Wall. Flying foot. Bed frame. Tentacle fingers. Hair. Fuck. Fuck. Open hand. Wall. Floor. Fuck.

I looked at myself in the mirror and began to wipe up the trails of mascara.

"All I wanted was to fucking eat some food," I said angrily, as if my emotions were a separate entity and I could shame them with my hunger.

LATER, I WENT back to my room to attempt some homework that the psychiatrist had assigned. Write down all of the negative thoughts I have in a day. Counter the negative thoughts with a positive thought.

Now, before doing this homework I had dabbled in affirmations and the power of positive thinking. Shit, I've watched the movie and read that well-known self-help book *The Secret*. I've made vision boards filled with images of things I wished to accomplish and achieve. Sitting in rehab wasn't one of the revelatory experiences I was trying to manifest. I've made all sorts of attempts at self-improvement. My mind had to be my strongest attribute. I was smart. It was something inside of me that was broken, not my mind.

I was wrong.

Being intelligent does not mean you don't have an asshole living inside your head.

Toting around a notebook to record every single negative thought is tedious. But I did get to meet the devious bastards who were bringing the ruckus. Apparently I have several dozen writers in my head. They are fueled on coffee and cocaine and are committed to scheming up crippling thoughts, self-sabotaging ideas, and unfounded fears.

They just never fucking tire.

When I did not have paper on hand, I would scrawl out my thoughts on napkins, receipts, or anything else that was available. I tucked hate-filled notes into my pockets and workbooks with worry that one piece might slip out for another person to pick up and read. They would see how messed up I am. But they were there too. We were all living cautionary tales.

Napkin #1: *Why do I have to fucking cry? Such a big fucking baby. Put a smile on your face and shut the fuck up.*

Notebook, line 6: *You did this to yourself. All of it.*

Notebook, line 8: *You're so fucking weak it makes me sick.*

Napkin #2: *I'm a fucking loser. Can't get shit right, might never get it right.*

Torn Paper #1: *It's pathetic when you cry. Everything is all your fault, you know that.*

Notebook, line 9: *Just give up already. It's in you to fuck everything up. Give up.*

I really didn't know how sick my mental state was until I took note of it. Literally, took notes of it. It shocked me and scared me. My mind was a monster and my mental health was its prey. So I began to counter the black-hearted beast with truths like "I have a right to my emotions," which seems simple enough but helped me profoundly.

When you have a lifetime of emotions that you have been running from, it seems like once they catch up they will gang-beat you and leave you crippled in an alleyway. Curb stomp finale. You learn to have distaste for them, to ignore their presence, and to dislike when other people are emotional. You learn to interpret their vulnerability as weakness and witnessing a sob might very well make your stomach churn. "Get it together," you'll mutter under your breath or in the back of your mind as other people weep. Seeing their emotion only reminds you of your own weakness, which in fact is not really a weakness at all but a necessity to live an emotionally healthy life. I continued to practise tracking, and my rebuttals started to happen naturally and I could stop my emotional-assholes in their tracks and allow room for myself to cry.

This writing assignment helped me to understand that I'd been terrified of emotions that couldn't do me any physical harm. I had a right to my emotions and had to fight with the assholes in my head to create space for me to feel them.

Notebook, line 12: *There is something wrong with you. You made everything happen. You're a drunk. You deserved it. Sluts can't get raped.*

New mantra: *No one has a right to hurt me. Not ever. No matter what.*

twelve

THAT WRITING ASSIGNMENT ISN'T THE ONLY THING
I faced with a feeling of dread over that week. I knew my
meeting with the gynecologist was approaching quickly.

The day had come.

It was raining out when I left the treatment centre to
head to the medical office in the town of Vernon. I thought
about how fitting it was that the great Mother Earth was
crying and cleansing with me. The thought comforted me
and wrapped itself around me as I buckled myself into the
passenger seat. I was nervous and doodled in my journal for
the first half of the journey before my nerves pushed me to
small talk with Cecelia, the client-service worker driving me.

The small talk was a diversion to keep me from thinking
about where we were going. Cecelia was a small, timid Indigenous woman with long hair that grey and white had taken

over. I discovered that Cecilia had no kids, was partial to classical music, and had an affinity for Asian-based fiction.

I felt excited and sick at the same time as we pulled up to the medical clinic parking lot and Cecelia turned off the ignition.

"I'll walk ya," Cecelia said, as if she had any other choice. You can't let addicts run loose in the city on their own. That's how corner drug-pushers fill their pockets and beer drains from the barkeep's taps.

"Do you suppose after my appointment I could get a cup of coffee?" I asked. The coffee back at the centre was black sludge and I needed a dose of caffeine and lots of nicotine to ease my jitters. Cecelia nodded. I felt like a child.

We found the office easily enough and Cecelia told me she would be downstairs when I was done. I wanted to ask her to wait with me and sit beside me like my mama would. I wanted her to hold my hand and squeeze it when my name was called to give me that extra push and sense of safety. Instead, I just nodded at her and sat in the pale blue waiting room. I kept my mind busy scanning the pictures of healthy communities and reminders for checkups on the wall.

I needed some way to stay focused on something other than my anxiety, which was threatening to overtake thoughts of reason. Yes, it would be awkward to spread my legs for a total stranger—especially since the rape. I was terrified. I had prepared myself in the months before to die alone with the shame of violent men between my legs.

My war-torn vagina.

My vagina comes with an introduction.

My vagina has a historical record of its own.

Life and death have lived here.

Men have spilled blood here.

My vagina and I fear we must disguise ourselves as something we are not . . . to find peace.

I had called my mom the night before. I needed to hear her soft voice and comforting words, to give me enough strength to make it through this appointment.

I cried in the client-service worker's office, where the only phone existed and privacy did not. The client-service worker on shift sat across the desk from me, pretending not to listen.

"Mama, I just want to fall into your arms," I whispered through my tears.

My mother's arms are like ancient fleshy tree limbs. Every time she wraps me in them, I feel safe. They are old wisdom and comfort.

"What's happening, my girl?"

"I have to go to the gynecologist tomorrow."

"For what?"

"For when . . . for when those men cut me. I have to make sure everything is okay."

"What men? What do you mean?"

"Mama, that happened back in December. I thought I told you. Mama, I'm scared—what if I can't have babies again?"

"Oh my girl," my mom's voice cracked, "I didn't know."

"One more minute," the client-service worker ordered. I never liked the guy. His voice was too high-pitched for the level of power he tries to wield with it. Old. Balding. Glasses. Smirky. I can see him being a social pariah on the outside of these walls. He gave me the creeps. Truth be told, most men his age give me the creeps. He was legitimately creepy, though.

I mentioned this to one of my counsellors. That I don't like being around older men because they remind me of the men who've caused me harm. I feel guilty in their presence. I shrink myself around them so they do not feel encouraged to cross boundaries. I become half a woman in the presence of men's insatiable appetites. The counsellor told me there is a name for this. It's called transference. That when a person or situation reminds you of historical events or individuals, the feelings attached to them cause emotions and behaviours to bubble to the surface.

But for this moment I put that aside. I needed to know that I am loved and supported.

"Mama, I love you. I gotta go," I whispered.

"I love you too . . ."

Confiding in my mom gave me the strength to be brave.

I fiddled with my fingers in the gynecologist's waiting room until my name was called. My doctor back in Fort St. John is originally from South Africa. Whenever pap-smear season comes around I am wriggling on the examination table trying to imagine being anywhere but there.

"Are there lions where you're from?" I'd ask, eyes clenched, with my feet in the stirrups.

I never await her reply, either. I keep asking more nonsense questions until the whole business with my downstairs is over.

"Tell me about the hippos . . ." I ask.

By the time I work my way to the zebras we are done and I am free to put my pants on.

There will be no talk of elephants today.

The gynecologist was a young woman, maybe six or seven years older than I, with a calm demeanour, and she spoke her words gently. We sat at a small table in her examination room. She created space for me to talk for a great deal of time about why I was there before any undressing was implicated. She was so kind and understanding. This was hard for the Indian girl in me who believed it was all her fault.

"That is terrible to hear, Helen. I have no idea what that must be like," she said softly, as she placed her hand over mine, her brown eyes glossed over.

When I cried I felt like I should have held back the tears. A part of me wanted to tell her that I was the one to blame and she shouldn't be so nice to me. She should see through me, I thought; she should scribble on a notepad and pin me down with a gaze of contempt. That didn't happen. I felt like an imposter. It was then that I realized it was only me judging myself there.

I remembered my mantra: *No one has the right to hurt me. Ever.*

She handed me Kleenex. "If you don't want to do this today, Helen, that is okay too," she said softly.

"No, no . . . I just want to get this over with," I answered.

She nodded and placed the garments I was to change into on the table and excused herself. I undressed slowly, feeling sorry for myself and then scolding myself for feeling sorry. I could never win with the assholes in my head. I lay on the exam table and the doctor came back in. Her voice drifted in and out as I focused on a spot on the wall trying to imagine lions and tigers and hippos.

"I see what you mean," her voice came from between my legs. "It's okay though, Helen. You don't need reconstructive surgery, it's healed up quite well. You have a healthy vagina."

After the appointment I walked downstairs to find poor unsuspecting Cecelia faithfully waiting for me, and we began walking to the car.

"Cecelia! Guess what?!" I exclaimed once we were on the sidewalk.

"What?" she said, turning her head.

"I have a healthy vagina!" I squealed loudly.

"Good for you," she replied casually, as if people made healthy-vagina comments on a daily basis. Cecelia had probably seen and heard it all, as she spent most of her waking moments around addicts.

Back at the treatment centre I had an appointment to discuss the results with my counsellor.

"I have a healthy vagina!" I squealed again, in her office.

"That's good, Helen. I am so happy. Remember when you were first sitting here? You didn't know if you could have children. Do you feel relieved?" she asked.

I nodded my head.

"You have been given this gift of health, now you must learn to honour it in a good way, Helen. Think about that."

I prayed that night that Creator and the grandmothers would show me how to honour myself, how to carry myself and to love myself. I prayed for healing for those who were still suffering from unspoken abuses and gave thanks for my healthy vagina.

It wasn't all happiness, though—my mind-beast was not satisfied with the relief that I felt. I opened up the notebook of negative thoughts and wrote, *You went and fucking bawled your eyes out like an idiot for nothing. You should feel stupid.*

I took a deep breath and wrote back to my mind-beast: *I was allowed to cry and feel scared of the outcomes. The event was traumatic for me. I am allowed to feel whatever I feel and right now I feel blessed with another chance.*

I shut the book and went to sleep that night feeling just a little lighter.

I was creating new trail ways for myself.

NOT LONG AFTER that news, sometime in the middle of my third week in treatment, my family made the twelve-hour trip to come visit me. Good behaviour and no disruptive incidents allowed me to go out on a weekend pass and be a self-monitoring individual. A taste of freedom. I squealed when they pulled into the parking lot. I ran outside and swept my son into my arms.

We visited the wildlife park in Kamloops. We ate ice cream under the shade of big trees. I laughed with him, cuddled with him, and held his tiny hand in mine.

"When you coming home, Mom?" he asked me as he licked the melting bubble-gum ice cream that dripped down his hand.

"In two weeks, Love. That's fourteen more sleeps! I know it seems like a long time but Mommy has been sick. There are people where I am staying that are helping me get better," I answered softly.

He looked at me with his light hazel eyes.

"I love you, baby. Mommy loves you to the moon and the stars. To haklay eenzah and suhn," I said as I ran my hand through his soft light brown hair.

"I love you too, Mommy," he said.

Once back at the hotel, we played superhero dress-up together. As the sun set on the first night, my mind began to buzz with the questions that my nightly journals had brought up. I needed hard answers and decided to question my mom after Mathias had gone to sleep. As we sat outside, nervous energy floated around us.

"Mom," my dry voice crackled and broke the silence, "you found out when I was thirteen about my childhood abuse. I was just wondering—I mean, I can't remember, did you try to take me to counselling or something? I mean, what did ya do?"

"That's not the first time I found out," Mom said.

"What?" I managed to whisper. My heart pounded. The background noise faded out.

Mom said to me, "That's not when it happened."

"What? Then when was it?"

Mom began to move uncomfortably on the hard cement picnic bench. She reached for a cigarette and looked past me, through me, to a moment hanging on to me like a shadow.

"You were two years old," she said, sucking back a drag. "I noticed some irritation around your privates so I took you to the doctor immediately. Sure enough the doctor confirmed that someone had done something to you. Rough rubbing and stuff happened." She paused and shifted her eyes toward the ground, then looked at me.

"After that we watched you closely, kept you away from him. I didn't know anything else happened after that until your friend told me when you were thirteen," she said with a nervous jump in her voice.

The *him* was my uncle. The uncle that my grandma took in as her own when he was a baby. The him who has pretty severe fetal alcohol syndrome and schizophrenia. He was a sexual predator. He abused me. He abused others.

He still came to family functions until I was in my early twenties. He'd always force his hugs on me and made my skin crawl when he held me for too long. I had forgiven him for his trespasses and for making my childhood a place from which I couldn't retrieve good memories. I was too scared to venture into my sexually warped childhood to find the good parts. Only when another family member became suicidal and drowned in addictions because of all of the abuse they suffered as a child did he finally get banned from family functions. It took years of unwanted hugs and forced silence for him to go away.

To this day my asu will preach the forgiveness that is found in the Bible when she talks about him. I can forgive him for fucking up my life. I will never forgive him for hurting those I love the most. I somehow missed the scripture that reads *Forgive your sexual abuser and let him eat at family dinners* when I was in Sunday school. As far as I know, he now lives in an extended-care home and requires constant medical attention.

I wasn't angry with Mom, but I wished she would've told me this a long time ago. It reinforced that we come from a family that doesn't talk about old bones and ruins from raging fires long forgotten.

I had another abuser too. She was five years older than me and her family often visited ours overnight. I remember how uncomfortable it was to watch her little sister play with Barbies. She would lay them on top of each other and simulate them having sex. It made me think that they were both abused and maybe that's why she thought it was normal to harm others.

"Barbies aren't supposed to do that," I said as she'd hold the dolls together.

"What do you know?" the little sister said.

I shared the bunk bed in my room with the older sister. I can remember only flashes from whatever took place at night. Her hands on me. Her mouth on my vagina. Me having to do the same to her. I was in Grade 2.

I never shared that ordeal in discussions with my mom. Things that were difficult to bring up were left in the shadows. I learned this dysfunctional pattern of keeping quiet when I was thirteen and went to stay the night at one of my aunties' homes. The aunties were always good at being second mothers, but they made some horrible choices when it came to men.

Her then boyfriend had caught me trying to make a pop can into a pipe to smoke some pot. He vowed not to tell my auntie and said he could even probably score me some weed.

"Sweet," I said, wanting the awkward conversation to be over so I could smoke my pot.

The next day, he came in to the bedroom with a bag of weed in his hand. He was a big, muscular Native man with an ear piercing and a foul mouth.

"Here," he said, stretching out his long brown arm.

I took the bag from his hand. "Thanks."

"Yeah, it's some real good shit," he said.

"Cool," I said.

"Your auntie is outside mowing the lawn right now." He nodded toward the back of the house.

"Okay," I answered, not knowing what to say to him.

"So can I have a kiss then? As a thank you?" he asked me as he came close enough to me that I could smell the beer on his breath.

"No. No. I'm not kissing you," I said, panic rising in my voice.

He reached to touch me and I hit his hand away.

"Whatever then. You fuckin' owe me," he barked at me as he stormed out and slammed the door. I sat frozen in fear and jolted when the door swung open again. "And don't be tellin' your fuckin' auntie about this," he said, his big brown finger inches from my face.

I nodded my head and he left the room.

I snuck the phone from the kitchen and called my dad. I was crying and asked him to pick me up. When I got home I told the story to my mom. She called my auntie—but there was no outrage. The next day, I got a very nice bouquet of flowers and a card from my auntie and her boyfriend.

It was a misunderstanding.
Uncle loves you.

I don't know what hurt me more. That no one seemed to care? Or that my auntie had written the card herself?

I fully understood silence.

Events involving other boyfriends of aunties and male family friends happened repeatedly to me. No one was there to protect me and I wanted to save myself the shame of ever receiving another card like that. So I never said anything.

Boundaries being crossed by men in authoritative positions became too normal for me. I learned who to stay away from. I held onto these secrets and lived with them. There was no one there in my corner to tell me that it was these men who were wrong.

But, sitting under that night sky with my mom, I resolved to never be quiet ever again. I was there to ask questions, to gain insight, and to move on. My dad didn't escape my questioning that night either. After my mom went inside, I called him out to join me. My poor family had come for a nice visit and got grilled instead. But it was all in the name of healing.

"All those times when Mama was drunk and angry—you left. How come you never took us?"

"What do you mean?" he asked.

"I mean once the fighting started you would take off," I said.

I could still hear the sound of his keys and the slamming of the door. Sometimes I would stare at the door longingly, waiting for him to come back for us, but he never did.

"Yeah, I didn't want to fight with your mom," my dad admitted.

"How come you never took us? When you left she was still angry and then she turned that on me."

"I . . . I . . ." my father stammered, "I thought that once I left, it stopped. It always seemed to be me that she was angry at." He lowered his head.

"I don't want to guilt you," I reasoned, "but I just never understood how you could leave us there like that. You didn't protect us and we were so young."

"I'm sorry, my girl," he said with tears rolling down his face.

"I know, Dad. I know," I said, placing my arm on his back.

IT WAS NOT easy to unearth past hurts like that, but I am glad I did it. It cleared the air and the rest of our visit went smoothly, like one of those normal families.

When I returned to the treatment centre, my next step was to relive all of my experiences and truly allow myself to cry and grieve for my body and spirit. I had to revisit every incident in my life and go through this process. It was frustrating, hard, and scary, but I knew that this guilt and shame was holding me back from being a warrior—for myself and for my son.

I wrote letters to myself at each age of abuse. I wrote letters to my attackers. I cried into my pillows and then I burned the letters with an offering of tobacco. In doing so, I gave my grief away.

thirteen

DURING THIS HEALING PROCESS, ONE OF THE PLACES I had to time-travel back to had happened years before. It was summertime and I was seventeen years old. The northern sun stayed out long and beat down hard. I pulled a few months sober out of a top hat and managed to keep a steady job.

I worked twelve-hour days, six days a week, doing traffic control on a reserve an hour outside of town. Every morning, I dragged myself into the work truck toting my thermos full of coffee. The two older women who claimed driver and front seat would play Ace of Base relentlessly on every single morning drive. They had a full-on air band orchestrated between the two of them. Hands became the reflection of the beats, bodies shook at high tempos. At first, it was comical, but when I realized a week into the job that the routine would not wear off, I slipped my earbuds in and drifted into my own world until we arrived at the work site. There must have been forty of us on that job, all but five of whom were men.

Every Monday morning, we circled around the foreman in the dusty equipment-laydown area. After I received morning orders, I stood in my chosen spot dutifully, stopping and releasing traffic when necessary. I had the simple job of making sure that the roadways stayed safe for public motorists as they navigated the fifteen or so kilometres of construction.

No one kept it safe for us, though.

I had traffic-controlled as a job the year prior and had already run into a gamut of experiences. Old men, twice my age, would grab at their crotches, mimicking what they wanted to do to me. Young men would start winking, blowing kisses, or catcalling. I complained once about someone making lewd gestures at me—he had grabbed his cock and gyrated in my direction. But the foreman didn't want to be bothered by my tits and their complaints.

I kept to myself and tried to make it through each day.

One old Native guy with shaggy hair and big quarter eyes, who smelled like cigarette smoke, would always get out of his excavator when he was working near me. I would curse under my breath as I watched his awkward gait and lean frame approach me. Once he was close, he would stare at me with an intensity that I could only equate to ill intentions.

"So how old are you again?" he asked as he pulled a cigarette from his yellow work vest pocket.

"Seventeen," I answered, turning away from him and kicking at rocks.

"Seventeen? I can't believe it. I thought you were a bit older than that," he said as he tilted his head sideways as if to take me all in with his gaze.

"Yup, really seventeen," I said, shaking my head slightly and refusing to look toward him again.

"Well, beautiful, break is almost over. I'll talk to you later."

I nodded my head and said nothing. Our interactions were always him forcing awkward questions on me, followed by my one-to-three-word replies. He knew I squirmed under his gaze and the weight of his sentences. He knew it and he liked it. I didn't know how to stop these encounters or how to voice that he was creepy. My voice was still unsure at that time of how to manifest itself to create boundaries. But finally I had enough and decided I would say something.

He made his way toward me, puffing on his cigarette, and stood there lurking.

"You're so pretty," he said, his eyes molesting my body.

"Uncomfortable!" I yelped loud and fast.

"What?" he said, a confused look on his face.

"Uncomfortable. I'm uncomfortable right now," I said and resumed staring at my boots.

He walked away. Sure, I didn't call him on his behaviour or make any strong and bold feminist declarations that day, but it was the start of me using my voice.

A FEW MONTHS into the job, a young fellow who was a couple years older than me pulled over in his gigantic rock truck. He opened the door and gazed down at me with a smile on his face. He was kind of handsome but not my type. He drove a huge jacked-up truck and blared his music every morning. He wore shiny shades and shiny shirts.

"You wanna go for a ride?"

He seemed nice enough and the idea of seeing the work site from an elevated perch intrigued me.

"Sure," I said as I placed my bags to the side of the road and climbed up the ladder and into the small driver's area.

"Wanna play with my stick while you're at it?" he said smartly as we took off down the dirt road.

"Uh . . . no," I answered as I shifted my body away from him.

"Ah, c'mon, it was just a joke. Loosen up," he said playfully.

I stared out at the road, at the deep gashes that the excavator had dug up, and imagined what the finished roadway would look like.

"You know I live out here, right?" he said as we turned down the road where the trucks dumped their haul.

"Yup."

"Well, just like I told that other girl, if you want to stay out here with me sometimes, you can. It must be tough driving back and forth every day."

"Really?"

"Yeah. I don't mind. I'll even drive you to work!"

"Ha ha—it's not a gentleman thing to do when you work at the same place," I laughed and started to feel more comfortable.

"Well, think about it. The offer is there if you want."

"Will do," I said as we drove back toward my original spot.

A week later, I found out that one of the girls in my crew had stayed at his place. I envied the ability to sleep for an extra hour in the morning. So, I asked her if it was safe to stay with him. Did she feel uncomfortable? She just shrugged her shoulders but had no complaints or concerns.

If I had to spend another morning listening to Ace of Base I was going to lose my mind. I waved his truck over just before the end of the day and he rolled down the window.

"Hey, I was thinking I could stay at your place tomorrow if that's still cool with you?" I asked.

"Yeah, for sure," he said with a smile on his face.

"All right, cool, I'll see you tomorrow then," I said. I stepped back and gave him a nod from under my orange construction helmet. He waved his hand and revved his engine, leaving a trail of dust behind him.

The following workday, he waited for me in the laydown area. Loud music blared from his stereo system. I jumped in.

"Now, my place ain't much but it's enough," he said as we walked up the stairs and he opened the door.

There were empty beer cans cluttering up the countertop in the kitchen and some pictures of family on his fridge. He was your everyday guy, I thought.

"Just make yourself at home," he said as he threw his bag by the couch, "I'm going to go hop in the shower."

I nodded and lay down on one of the big brown sofas. I was looking forward to my turn to shower. The dust and grime of the day formed a layer on my skin, and to feel human after that, a shower was necessary.

I drifted off and woke up to the sound of cupboards closing in the kitchen.

"Shit, how long was I out for?" I asked groggily from the couch.

"Not too long, I figure I'd make you something to eat too," he said, and I heard a pan hissing on the stove.

"That's awesome. I still need a shower, though," I said as I sat up.

"Towels are at the end of the hall."

I grabbed my overnight bag and headed to the bathroom for my daily rebirth. After I got out of the shower, I examined what he had on his countertop. Mouthwash. Hair gel. Cologne that looked expensive. Needles.

Needles?

I stood frozen in place, trying to think of reasons for needles in his bathroom.

Diabetic?

I didn't think so.

Heroin?

Didn't really fit.

I pulled open a drawer and found a bottle of steroids. It made sense. He was a gigantic guy with a big frame and muscles. He bragged about running around the rez with a tire strapped to his back. I closed the drawer.

I felt unsafe.

"Supper's done," he called from the kitchen.

"Okay," I said as I came out of the bathroom still towel-drying my hair.

"Steak and salad good?"

"Thanks, that's great," I replied.

He couldn't be that dangerous, I thought, not when he's this nice.

After dinner he flicked on the television set and I felt myself starting to drift again.

"Where am I sleeping?" I asked. "Here on the couch?"

"Nah, in that bedroom over there." He pointed to the room beside the bathroom.

"All right, well, I gotta call it a night. I'm beat and am going to use that extra hour of sleep."

"Okay, I'm going to sleep soon too," he said.

I brushed my teeth, ignoring the syringes that lay by the sink. I went into the bedroom and slid under the covers. I was lying there for almost a half an hour when I heard him walk into the room.

"Uh . . . what are you doing?" I asked him.

"Going to sleep," he said gruffly.

"Where?"

"Right here. This is my bed," he said. When he noted the look of alarm on my face he added, "Relax. I'm using a different blanket. It's no big deal."

"Okay," I said and turned onto my side knowing it would be harder for me to sleep now with this big guy I barely knew beside me.

"Hey," he whispered.

"What?"

"Wanna cuddle?"

"Go to bed," I said like I was teasing. But I was scared. I didn't know how to say, *Go sleep elsewhere*. I didn't know how to say I was uncomfortable or wanted to go sleep on the couch. My body felt frozen to the spot.

Boundaries were still really new to me. A few months before, I finally had said no to sex for the first time. It took me two years of counselling to muster up the nerve to regain some control over my body.

I felt like I was trapped. I finally drifted off to sleep but only for a short time. I woke up to him dry humping my leg. My eyes grew wide in panic.

"What are you doing?" I said, fear making my voice shake.

"Come here," he said as he tried to pull me toward him.

"No, just go to bed, okay?"

"Just come over here," he said, grabbing my waist and pulling me into him. His erection pressed into my hip.

Needles. Steroids. Anger. I didn't want to make him mad.

"We have to get up in the morning. Remember I need that extra hour of sleep? Let's just go to bed, okay?" I said, trying to make it seem like sleep was a good idea.

As I pulled my blanket around me, my body trembled. Finally, when I thought he was sleeping, I drifted off again.

He woke me up a second time—when I felt a strange sensation near my anus. I realized his face was down there. He had pulled my pants down.

"What the fuck are you doing?" I shrieked as I pulled away and reached for my pants.

He pulled me quickly and hard into him.

"Just fuckin' come here," he said as he started to kiss my neck and hump my bare ass.

"No," I whimpered as I pulled my face away from his—I didn't want him to kiss my lips.

"Shhhh," he whispered as he continued to hump me.

He was stronger than me. He kept me pulled into him and his hands grabbed onto me and held me tightly until it hurt.

At seventeen I already knew what it was like to be raped. I know how it feels to have something taken from you.

He was going to take it.

He was going to take it no matter what.

If I fought, I knew he would get violent with me. Sometimes it's easier to just let it happen. I stopped resisting and my body went limp. His empty brown eyes stared into mine and he tried to kiss me. I turned my head to face the wall. He turned my head back to face him and tried to kiss me again. When his lips hit mine I started to cry and then I couldn't stop crying. He shoved himself into me a few more times until he climaxed with me crying underneath him. I was still crying softly and rolled over on my side when he stood up and went to go sleep on the couch.

In the morning, he brought me coffee in bed and tried to kiss me and play with my hair like a lover would. As if what he did was consensual.

I didn't talk to him that morning and I didn't say anything when we got to work.

I didn't say anything about that incident for years.

A year later I saw him out one night in an Alberta bar, just after my eighteenth birthday. He tried to talk to me and I had been drinking already. I shook my head at him and walked away.

"Go ahead and be a stunned cunt then!" he yelled after me. I turned around and ran at him, shoving him into a wall.

"Fuck you!" I screamed as my friends came and pulled me away from him.

"What was that about?" they questioned me.

"I . . . don't want to talk about it," I said as I downed my drink and walked to the bar to order a triple.

I had always blamed myself for that night. Whenever I looked back I started on the *why didn't I*s and *I should have*s.

I should have told him to sleep on the couch to begin with.

Why didn't I see that he was crazy in the first place?

Why didn't I call somebody?

I should have fought harder.

I should have called the police the next day.

I should have said *no* one more time.

New mantra: *No one has the right to harm me. Ever.*

I wrote a letter to my seventeen-year-old self. I would later burn this letter with a tobacco offering in a sacred fire so that Creator could hold onto the pain for me. In that note, I told my seventeen-year-old self that it wasn't her fault. I told her that she did the best she could, in the way that she knew how, to protect herself from him. I cried for her, howled into the pillow with snot flowing down my face for her. This process was not just about allowing myself to have feelings about what these men have done to me, but allowing myself to grieve for the pain and hate I directed toward myself at different ages. I was bravely coming to terms with all of the traumatic events in my life and allowing myself the space to feel. I was allowing myself to let go of the events and give them to Creator. The violence of men would no longer define my life for me.

I wanted to be free.

I wanted her to be free.

I HAVE ALWAYS had a hard time staying angry with someone, even those who have wronged me. I have tried to hold hate as a buffer from my own feelings but it never made sense to me. My time at the treatment centre helped me to see that holding onto this negative energy was something that attacked my very being. An intrusion of termites invading my home and crawling up the walls, refusing to remain small and unnoticed. I almost allowed that hate to eat the foundation out from under me.

I forgave everyone except myself.

I went for treatment that final time to heal fully. It was why I was so brave, but I didn't feel brave at the time. Healing isn't a freeing experience when you're in the middle of it. It feels like land mines are exploding and ripping your flesh apart. Everywhere you step is dangerous.

When I was writing the letters to myself to burn, I was in a continual state of emotional rubble. I would walk away from a conversation in mid-sentence because I could feel tears coming. I broke down multiple times a day for almost a week straight. I was a complete wreck.

I survived it. It did not kill me to feel all of my emotions.

One exercise we did was on forgiveness. I was instructed to write a letter to someone who has harmed me. In this letter, I was to state how I'd been harmed and, in turn, talk about how I harmed myself.

The ending was about how to do things differently.

After we all wrote our letters, we dispersed into male and female groups. The women's group was located in the gym. As the overhead fluorescent lights buzzed, we placed white tea candles to mark our sharing circle. We all had to go up and share the words we'd written. But we also got to choose two other women to come up for support.

When it was my turn, I called on my two women. I didn't know what to expect from the group or myself. I stood before a half-dozen other clients and the three counsellors. My hands were shaking.

"I . . . I have never been able to forgive myself. I have always felt that it was always all my fault. I was sexually abused as a little girl and raped four times as a young woman. I have had family friends or men who dated my aunties try to seduce me. I always thought there was something wrong with me. There must have been something wrong with me. Some wrong part of me made all of those things happen. And even when I hear someone say it is not my fault, I can't believe them. I have hated myself for most of my life." Tears were flowing down my face. "The way that I punished myself was to believe I was worth nothing. I would drink to numb everything, destroy my chances at happiness, and never let anybody too close to me. I was always afraid they would tell me I was actually a bad person. I put myself in situations where people could harm me, hurt me, and then I hated myself even more. Then I would say, 'Look, Helen—look at what you fucking did to yourself.'"

I felt like I was choking on my words. All of my emotions became tangible creatures trying to escape out of me. I leaned over with my hands on my thighs, trying to regain balance. I crumpled my paper in my right hand.

The shame, pain, and anger all manifested as actual physical pain.

"Let it out," I heard a voice say.

I stomped my foot into the gym floor and screamed.

It was painful. I screamed again.

It was more howl than scream. More wail than howl.

It was all of these things escaping from my mouth.

I was calling my spirit back into my being.

I was pushing all of the shit out to make space for remembering who I am.

"Breathe, Helen, breathe," I heard the voice of my counsellor instruct me.

One of the women placed her hand on my back and I stood up.

"I forgive myself," I said, my breathing shaky. "From now on I will not punish myself. I will love myself and know that I am worth something. I am a good person and will not hurt myself anymore."

After twenty-four years I finally did it. I forgave myself and meant it.

A SWEAT LODGE ceremony was planned for later that day. We were to burn our letters with a tobacco offering to cleanse. My counsellor was an older woman, probably in her late sixties. She may have had a small frame, but there was a fierceness about her that you didn't want to provoke.

She pulled me aside, "Helen," she said, "I want you to come with me and we will prepare a medicine for you to cleanse with today."

I nodded and followed her toward the lodge.

She instructed me to start a small fire in the firepit that was near the lodge. I gathered small sticks and grabbed a few logs, just like Asu had taught me when I was a little girl. The process of gathering and stacking was meditative for me. It held warm and familiar memories.

We placed a heavy silver pot that was filled with water on the metal grate that sat over the fire.

"Place these in there," my counsellor said as she handed me juniper, rosehips, and other medicines. I put them in the pot. "Today, after the sweat, I want you to stay behind. You are going to wash yourself with this medicine, Helen. I brought cedar boughs for you to brush yourself off," she said.

"Okay," I said.

"The other women will be here soon to the build the fire for the sweat rocks. Stay here until they come," she instructed and I nodded.

I felt like a small girl in this moment. I didn't know any of these cultural practices, given that they were teachings from another tribe. But I was always grateful when somebody shared their knowledge. I sat on the wooden bench and stared into the fire.

After we finished our four rounds of prayer in the Sweat Lodge, we burned our letters in the fire. Most made their way back to the residence. I stayed behind with my counsellor, as instructed. She filled a small pail with the medicine water and handed it to me.

"Take that into the lodge and I will grab you the cedar boughs," she said gruffly.

I placed the pail inside the lodge and crawled back in.

The lodge is like the womb. When we are in it, we are close to Mother Earth and Creator. All of the elements work together so that we can cleanse and are able to pray there. The frame is made of willows. Grandfather rocks are placed in the centre pit, which is heated by fire. Water splashed onto the heated rock is what carries the steam that cleanses us.

I sat just inside the opening in the eastern side of the sweat.

"Here," my counsellor said, as she passed the boughs in. "I want you to pray while you are in here. Wash yourself with that medicine. Use the boughs to wipe yourself. Pray to cleanse your body and to give thanks for it. Your body is your own gift, Helen. This is a new start for you, a new journey. Say what you need to say and come out when you are finished," she said, a little softer than before. She closed the flaps to the door and left me to pray in solitude.

I washed. I prayed. I washed. I prayed.

This was my rebirth.

THAT NIGHT, I had a dream.

I was somewhere out in the universe and surrounded by stars. I felt connected to them. It felt like home. I saw a light purple cloud, thick but not solid. Somehow, I knew that cloud was me.

Then it went black.

There was a flash and a pair of moccasins appeared. I didn't recognize them and knew that they weren't mine. They weren't meant to be a part of my journey and they tried to push their way into my purple substance. They tried to push their way into my being. That pushing was relentless and I knew I had to fight whatever thing was behind these moccasins.

Everything went black and a battle ensued.

I was fighting for my life and I could feel the struggle magnify as the vibrations grew stronger. I summoned my voice, telling whatever I was fighting with, "I have strong medicine."

The fight stopped and I won whatever unseen battle this may have been. My eyes opened. I could still feel the dream trying to pull me back into sleep. I only had the functioning use of the right side of my body. My left side still buzzed and vibrated and I couldn't move it. I managed to throw my right arm across my body and pulled the left side of my body until I was sitting upright and the dream left me alone.

There are unexplainable things in the dream world.

I was rattled and did not want to fall back asleep right away. I was scared I would be taken to the same dream. I thought about what just happened.

I have strong medicine?

I don't talk like that, I thought.

I knew I'd have trouble getting back to sleep so I went and asked a client-service worker to smudge out my room.

As sage smoke filled the air, I prayed some more.

I tried to relax and go back to sleep, but I kept thinking of those moccasins. They weren't mine and they weren't a good feeling. They wanted me, to take over my journey again, but I fought it and I won. I had won my life back.

I am in my own moccasins now.

fourteen

ON MY THREE-YEAR SOBRIETY MARK, I PACKED MY bags and tossed them to the back of my car. I was on a continual journey forward and I was excited. I could feel the anticipation in my stomach as I readied myself to embark on a bold new adventure.

I'd already worked toward and received my bachelor's degree in social work. It's the reason my uncle gave me a car. A silver pony with a missing hubcap.

I'd awoken early on that morning of my graduation ceremony. I held my sleeping son, and I reflected on how far we had come and how well we have been since my last time in treatment. And even through all that turmoil—of struggling through school, of close encounters with relapse—I somehow knew we'd make it.

I promised him when he was born that we were going to make it. I told myself this as I scrubbed urinals and desks, years ago. Mathias was barely one year old when I knew we were going to have a good life. When he was born, nine pounds and five ounces, we had no money but his mama had hope.

We were finally on the road to a hopeful future filled with opportunity.

As for my next step, I'd be on the road soon too, to Edmonton. A city I have learned to see in a different light since the darkness has left me.

I have had some really amazing things happen in my life, things that continue to put me in a space of awe and humility. As these events take place I silently acknowledge that, with everything I have been through, I'm not even supposed to be alive. But I am, so I tell myself to be grateful, be humble, be real, and do good things.

So, I was headed back to Edmonton. The city where I almost lost myself in blurred lines of cocaine while I was spinning in circles. I had been given the chance to create my own space of healing—for others. I had found my voice.

I had applied for and received an arts grant to make two poetry videos that focused on ending violence against Indigenous women. They were to be filmed in Edmonton. I wasn't spinning in circles anymore, but coming full circle.

Small things had to happen for bigger things to follow suit. It started from a blog that I wrote while in my third year of the social work program in Merritt, British Columbia.

That's how I met Cheyenne, a Métis filmmaker who followed my writing. The blog was called *Reclaim the Warrior*. It was dedicated to processing and sharing my decolonization journey. Cheyenne emailed me and asked to use one of my older poems for a small video. I said yes, and who knew I was opening the door to larger projects and ultimately to a woman I would eventually think of as a sister.

The main focus of the project was the poem "The Things We Taught Our Daughters." It was a culmination of my healing journey, countless conversations, and reflection on violence in Indigenous communities in both urban and rural settings. I realized more and more as I held space for other women over the years how pervasive silence is. The more I shared stories with Indigenous women across the country, the more I realized how common some of my experiences were. There are women out there holding onto these stories without ever letting them see the light. I wanted to be brave, not only for me, but to help create some change for them.

THE THINGS WE TAUGHT OUR DAUGHTERS

Sometimes we taught them silence
to let the secrets stay on their lips

Sometimes we taught them to look away
to forget and not bear witness

We showed them how
to play hide and seek
with historical afflictions
to pretend that the monsters from the closet
didn't escape. Don't exist. Are not real.
Sometimes to protect our own wounds
we forced our daughters not to feel

Maybe we were taught this ourselves
If you focus hard enough on forgetting
You can live through any kind of hell
Hush. Quiet Now. That's enough, my girl.
Silence.

Fat lips and bruised eyes
Say more than the mouth will tell you
Show less than what the eyes have seen
It didn't happen. Forget about it. He didn't mean it.
We don't call the police on our own.
Just learn to stay away . . . Stay Away. Stay
Away

Somewhere we learned how to create an asylum
for the very things
that plague our dreams
Somewhere we learned blind eyes
      and buried skeletons

provide just enough relief
to live just enough
without ever really living

We stuck sexual abuse up on the mantelpiece
Picture-framed the portrait of rape
and named the old rez dog Domestic Dispute

We gave all of this shit a home
the aggressive interloper intrudes
and we accepted its right to exist
Love just isn't really love
if he doesn't say it with his fists
Enough now. Quiet. He didn't mean to.
They would never hurt you like that.
Your uncle, he loves you.

Our inaction translating to
another generation
accepting the presence of violations
When we were little girls
We should have slept safely in our beds
Mothers should have said

My girl, you are worth a thousand horses
and any man
would give a thousand more

We would know the phrases
Speak up. It is never your fault. No means no.
You have the birthright to be free from harm,
and any man who would violate these
        treaties between bodies
would be dealt with by the women.
Because we protect our own,
even if this means calling the police on our own.

Because my girl,
You are sacred, valuable, indispensable,
        and irreplaceable
This is what needs to be said, needs to
        be shown, needs to be told.

Because our daughters . . .
Will one day grow old
and maybe they'll be women
with short-term memories
practising daily burial ceremonies
focused on forgetting.

It is time to remember.
Time to summon our voices from
        the belly of the earth.
Time to feel, cry, rage, heal, and to
        truly live life instead.
It is time to tell ourselves and our daughters,
the things that should have been said

PART THREE: THE HEALING

The words I had written spoke to Cheyenne, and the poem immediately became the main focus of our collaboration.

But, just before I left for Edmonton, there was an unforeseen twist to the project that gave me pause. Cheyenne no longer wanted just to use my words and voice to narrate it. She asked me to be present in the video and not just the voice of it. I hesitated. I called my mama, who had become an anchor for me in my sobriety and healing.

"Do you know what this means?" I said to my mom on the phone later that night.

"What?" she asked.

"I'll be the face of sexual abuse and violence experienced by Indigenous women."

"And?"

"Mama, if I do this, I'm going to be single for the rest of my life," I said before I started laughing at the real possibility of it.

"No, you won't!" my mama said. She was supportive, the way a mom is supposed to be. We laughed together, and she added, "Oh well, the things you know need to be said."

And it was decided. Or rather, Creator decided a path for me and I paid attention for the signs and moved when I was supposed to. I trusted that I would be taken care of.

I am taken care of.

Still, the thought of reading my poem in front of a camera and to a room full of strangers made my stomach tighten. It wasn't a new sensation. Reading my poetry in public has always frightened me. I remember the first time.

It was years ago, after returning from my first trip to Nicaragua. A community event was being held at a local coffee shop. My boss at the time had asked me to read poetry with her at this event as part of an International Women's Day celebration.

"I'm not doing it," I told my best friend Kyla.

"Why not?" she asked.

"Poetry is different. What if nobody likes it?"

"Who cares if they don't? But you know as well as I that you're a damn good writer. Just do it."

"But . . ." I hesitated.

"But what?" She was still trying to convince me.

"I'm scared shitless," I had to admit.

"Don't you always tell me that if there is fear there is room for growth? So if you're scared that's a good thing. You'll grow from it. You have to do it."

I grimaced. All that self-help-book talk came back to bite me in the ass and was forcing me to display my innards to a crowd of strangers. Poetry, and reading poetry to strangers, has always been different for me because my words are a part of me. Sharing words that I've written with people has another level of vulnerability that I still sometimes struggle with. It is me baring my soul with each stanza to a room full of people I will never know on a first-name basis.

But Kyla talked me into it. And so I stood there, on International Women's Day, about to recite my own words to the public for the first time.

When they called my name, I asked my boss to stand beside me in support. Women have always been there to support me, to help me on my journey. She placed her hand on my back as if to absorb some of the nervous energy that coursed through my being.

I used to have a bad lip quiver anytime I was nervous presenting to a crowd. Back then, the lip quiver was in full effect and I heard the girl in the front row comment to her friend, "Why is her lip shaking?"

That. Damned. Quivering. Lip.

I'd gone to Toastmasters a few years before, hoping to develop the confidence to get rid of it. It didn't help, and I struggled through that first reading.

I survived it.

It scared me.

And I did it again. I read in public again. And again.

Sometimes my knees still quake, even today. But I left that lip quiver behind me.

But each time on stage is different. And each poem opens up a different kind of vulnerability. Each time I have to tell myself to be brave.

I hoped that my legs wouldn't quake and I would remember my lines for this film project.

Indeed, during my long drive to Edmonton I tried to sort through the anxieties and fears that surrounded my performing in front of a camera and film crew. I practised my lines for most of the eight hours of the drive. My mind still ran a little rampant but I tried to let the fears go.

What if they expect me to be some epic spoken-word artist and have all my stuff memorized?

What if they are disappointed?

What if my lip quiver comes back?

I knew I'd be required to stand in front of a room full of strangers and declare that I have been sexually abused and raped.

I almost turned my car around several times before finally arriving at the film set.

What did I get myself into?

That's it . . . I'm fucking crazy.

Okay. Okay. I got this. Pray. Trust. Breathe.

The grandmothers must have been travelling with me. I found the courage to do this project.

There were seven people in that film crew. They set up the lighting and backdrop while I stood outside and rehearsed with Faye. She was a production assistant and part of her job was to make sure I felt comfortable. Faye was a long-haired and beautiful Haida woman with a gentle spirit. She cued me when I needed it and gave me encouragement when I faltered. "One more time," she'd say, as we sat outside on a wooden bench, the sun overhead and a breeze fluttering my papers. When rehearsal was finished, I excused myself. A found an empty room and called my mama.

Over the years of our sobriety, and a few really solid talks, my mom and I had healed our relationship. It didn't happen without a lot of work, a lot of forgiveness, and a lot of love. Mom became Mama again. She represents the roots that keep me grounded and the person who breathes life into me when I need it the most.

"Mama, we are about to start," I said.

"That's good, my girl," she replied.

"Mama?"

"Yes?"

"Will you pray with me?"

Pray. Trust. Breathe.

fifteen

EXCEPT FOR CHEYENNE AND FAYE, EVERYONE ON the film crew was white. It would be a lie if I said that didn't bother me. It would also be a lie if I said I didn't struggle at first because the content of what I had to share was so deeply personal. I thought I would have to repeat the poem a maximum of three times. I was severely disillusioned. There were several scenes and locations where I would have to read.

There were times when the words conjured experiences and memory. When that happened, it hit my body and I trembled, not out of nervousness, but out of remembrance. After the last take for the day, I excused myself to use the washroom. Once there and alone, my body curled into a question mark in the stall and I wept.

I didn't want to do this project to feel glamorous, to feel important, or to preach. I wanted to do it because

I believed it to be necessary to share with others. Being frank and open and honest in this way might encourage the healing journey for others. That was my hope. My mama's voice on the phone and her prayer reminded me of that purpose.

I used to believe that sexual abuse was exclusively an "Indian girl" experience when I was growing up. I remember when I met my first Indian girl at age fourteen who hadn't been sexually abused and I was so confused. I did not know that it was something that did not happen to all of us. I know that it isn't an experience shared by all Indian girls now, but I also know there are still many of us. I was brave for them. It took days to complete shooting this film. Once that process was over, there was still a great deal of post-production work to do.

Days later, the filmmaker and I sat on her couch wrapped in blankets. The time had come to screen and begin editing the material. I watched in awe as the video took shape. I overcame the awkwardness of watching myself on camera.

I was proud of the work that we had done.

When we finally finished editing and watched the un-mastered final, I began to cry again in gratitude. It was wild to be there on this side of healing. To perhaps inspire someone through poetry I have written. It was truly a pivotal moment in my journey.

And in that moment—it made me think of Her.

I wondered where she was? Was she safe?

Her. The teenaged friend I ran away to when I was thirteen. We'd both been in this city before. She was the first person who loved me in the middle of my shit—no questions asked.

When I was thirteen and told her, over a hollow receiver, that I had been raped, she began to hit her head against the wall. I can remember the thumping noise coming over the phone. My trauma seemed to hit her harder than her own did. I didn't understand that until I was seventeen and my little cousin told me over the telephone that she had been raped. My body curled inside itself, a howl birthed from my gut passed through my lips and I cried.

If only I could hold that pain for her, she could be all right. It's already happened to me. I could hold that pain for her. She could be all right, I thought.

I understood why she hit her head that night. She wanted to hold my pain for me.

She used to call me on my birthday; no matter where she was, she remembered to dial my number. Sometimes I'd awake to a 3:00 a.m. phone call with a semi-coherent Her on the other line, calling from a phone number I knew was some guy's and knew better than to call her back on.

"Happy birthday, my girl," she would say.

I looked forward to these once-a-year calls because then I knew she was alive. The other 364 days, I was used to having the worry. Would I receive another birthday phone call? Or, would I come to learn that a violent pimp or john had taken her life? Would I someday find out that the drugs had finally claimed her heart? I changed my number one year, without thinking about Her and how she'd memorized the number I had for years. I cut off our lifeline and we lost connection.

I talked to my mom on the phone one night after we finished shooting. I mentioned Her and said I wanted to go search for her.

"Apparently, Helen . . . her mom told the family that she has been sick for a while now. I don't know what it is, but I know it's bad, Helen, really bad."

Hollow receiver.

I had always held onto the hope that we would both be sober together. Healed up and whole. That we would be able to grow into old kohkums together with a hell of a story to tell. I could see us, aged and holding hands on a porch, watching a sunset and doing old-people things.

But, this was reality. This was the truth I didn't want to face, that maybe she will never get sober, that maybe her addictions will rule her and she will become sicker and sicker until there is no longer a chance.

"Mama," I cried, "she's going to fuckin' die on those streets if she doesn't take care of herself!"

"I know, my girl, I know," my mama said.

I wanted to find Her. Not to tell her that she needs to sober up and take care of herself. She already knows that. All addicts know that. I wanted to find her to tell her that I love her, that I have always loved her and that I always will. I have carried around the weight of worry and sadness for her since I was thirteen years old.

In the beginning of my sobriety I had wondered why I was given healing and not her.

Our work on the film was finished and I spent my last night in Edmonton driving up and down 118 Avenue in search of Her. I paid special attention to the streets where I thought she might be hanging out. I spent hours smoking cigarettes and drinking too much coffee—going this way and that way—hoping to catch a glimpse of Her.

Nothing.

I cold-called phone numbers of random men whom I was told she sometimes used as a safe place. Each time, it turned up a dead end. I finally gave up trying to find Her and returned to my uncle's place where I was staying. As I lay on my bed that last night in Edmonton, my thoughts kept going to Her. Then my thoughts became a prayer.

A prayer for Her and countless others who remain stuck on the black road of addiction. I knew that if I was to truly honour Her and my gift of sobriety, I needed to live. To truly live with a fierceness and tenacity unmatched.

I would try to fit two lifetimes into one.

I would try to do justice by the lives we were given and create justice for what our lives have lost.

I would do the things that scared me.

I would have the audacity to dream bigger and be bolder.

I would accomplish things that the world told us was out of our reach.

Each step I take in sobriety is ceremony.

This life is a sacred pilgrimage.

I carry Her with me.

I carry Her into the Sweat Lodge.

I carry Her with me as I dip my toes into different seas.

I carry Her with me into each new opportunity.

It prompted my memory to something that one of my professors said years ago. She once told me that the first part in trauma is where you find yourself a victim. The second is when you become a survivor. But to truly live, you move past that to what she called "being a thriver."

sixteen

IT WAS ASU WHO ALWAYS MANAGED TO FIND THE unseen blessings in every moment. Maybe now, after all of this chaos, I have finally figured it out. If I hadn't been lost, I may never have found the richness and strength and beauty of my own culture. I haven't done it alone. I've had so much help along the way. And that help? It always arrived just when I needed direction.

The first knowledge keeper who showed up was my school counsellor in junior high. He liked to speak in riddles.

"One day you are going to love your pain," I remember him saying as he picked up another rock, examined it slowly, then threw it into the river. I walked beside him quietly. He always said things that I didn't really understand, but this was one of the more far-fetched concepts he had tossed my way.

He kept his hair long, decorated by wisps of white. He always had his trademark jovial smile and donned a leather vest. Every Indian needs a good vest. My dad has a vest. One of my first Native boyfriends had a vest. Hell, even I have a bunch of vests.

I was grateful to have him in my life. He was one of the first males I had ever trusted and confided in. He made me realize that not everyone who gives something wants something in return. He never made me feel it was unsafe to discuss things that were difficult to say. He patiently waited for me to come to my own realizations. I gave him pieces of my struggle but never a full picture.

But one day, he pushed me too far. I wasn't ready for what he had to say.

"You realize that these are your choices? That you can stop it all by making the choice to stop it?"

I can't remember exactly what we were talking about, but it was likely my getting blackout drunk and sleeping with guys I didn't want to sleep with.

I was angry with him when he said that and I instantly shut down. I asked him to drop me back off at school and refused to visit with him again. Did he not know what happened to me? Did he not hear me all this time I'd been telling him all the shitty things that happened in my life? I was a fucking alcoholic with memories of sexual abuse that surfaced every single fucking day. How could I stay sober? How could I not go get blitzed with an alcoholic for a mom? He was supposed to fix me so I could not do this shit.

Control of my life was an illusion. I was that heavy silver pinball banging around in the game with someone else touching the buttons. Hit a button and I bounced all over the place until I sunk or got trapped in one of those little areas where the gate comes up. All my life, things out of my control had been happening to me, and my environment had made me believe that I was powerless.

You're just an Indian.

Ping. Ping. Ping.

Shitty things happen and they will always keep happening to you. Particularly because shitty things happen to people like you. Poor, broke, Indian girls with fucked-up pasts and addictions so strong they could pull the tide. Just learn to accept it.

Ping. Ping. Ping.

That is where I lived for a very long time. When I finally became sober and stayed sober, I realized I had achieved what I'd thought was impossible.

If I could become sober, something I had never thought I could do, then what else could I do? I began to reclaim pieces of my power that had been taken from me. I took back the power that I had given away because I thought it would just be taken from me if I didn't. I went back to school for my degree, I helped build schools in Nicaragua, I went to Switzerland, I went to Guatemala and sat in circle with Indigenous people impacted by mining.

I decided I would no longer believe in disempowerment and no control. I decided I would never again be silenced.

I started to realize that I could accomplish anything in life and that being powerless was the ultimate illusion.

Learned helplessness is what this feeling is called. How many of us, as Indigenous people, have continually—generation after generation—lived through events that have created a sense of powerlessness? Some still feel like this.

It all stems from history. Colonial oppression of Indigenous people did not stop a century or so ago. It continues today. The wielding of power and privilege is reaffirmed by the media and the majority of society. It is no wonder so many of us have forgotten our true power. We can look way back to the creation of reserves and how that created a dependency on outside sources to give us our basic needs.

The Pass System required Indians to get permission from their Indian agent to leave the reserve. It made it impossible to live, hunt, gather, trade, and basically do all the things we had always done in order to survive.

We can look at residential schools and how that legacy contributed to a learned helplessness. If you have read this book and know nothing about residential schools, you need to acquire that education for yourself. And please do so promptly.

There are many more policy-based, law-based actions that were targeted at Indigenous people in order to "assimilate" us. To clarify, *assimilate* is another word for "to fuck up emotionally, mentally, physically, and spiritually."

There are a lot of us who have lived through the accumulated shit storm caused by the generational traumas. All of these moves were calculated to "kill the Indian." And guess what? It didn't make any of us white, nor did it make us disappear. It just made a lot of us feel lost and broken.

There are parents who don't know how to parent.

There are people still silencing their own people.

Again, if you don't know about residential schools and thought they were something that happened a couple hundred years ago, please educate yourself. It should no longer be the responsibility of Indigenous people to do the work for you.

I have facilitated Intergenerational Trauma workshops in Indigenous communities. The majority of the people who attend are always the same type of person. We call those people community champions. The community champions are people who bear the heavy loads in communities. They are the ones to whom people go with their problems. They are the fixers and the solution seekers.

And, they are tired.

In those workshops, I always talk about the practice of self-care. You need to take care of yourself or you will not be able to help anyone. Without self-care, no one can assist families in need. They won't be able to help their cousin or niece find sobriety. Nor can they assist others to be healthy and strong.

Each of these is part of our collective mindset in our First Nations communities.

The collective mindset creates a desire to grow and move forward in a good way. But it cannot be done without doing self-work.

This is where I talk about reclaiming medicine.

When I was searching for my life's purpose, I was told to look backward and look for repetition. Look at the generations before you and see what was left undone. So I did. I saw that many of my family members were able to achieve sobriety but some went on "dry drunks." They replaced drink with gambling. Others look to different diversions like sex, anger, or shopping. Without self-examination, many still operate from their core hurts and clutch onto beliefs that cannot serve them well.

This is where I saw my purpose.

I came here to heal to the best of my ability and shift that generational transference.

Healing is not a solitary act.

When healing takes place, it has no other option but to ripple out. It ripples out from the individual into the family, into the community, into the Nation, and into the world. Our healing not only reaches forward to our future grandchildren, but it leans backward simultaneously and grasps the hands and hearts of our ancestors.

Our healing is the reclamation of medicine. We take back our power in this way. Never underestimate the act of healing yourself, and if the world around you is still struggling and individuals will not listen, just focus on that over which you do have control.

Healing yourself is a revolutionary act.

Healing yourself is the ultimate act of resistance.

Healing is the act of remembering who we are as Indigenous peoples. Healing is the act of undoing the years of trauma and shame that have been swept on top of us. Seeking healing is the bravest thing people can do. And when you choose to do it, you do not do it alone. We have ancestors who stand behind us. They wait for us to ask for their help and guidance. We all come from warriors. Remember this.

I have become grateful for my pain—just as that first school counsellor predicted. It has given me my heart for the people. I have learned to fill the chasms that trauma left behind with love.

I found a way to heal from my pain.

I believe I was given the task to heal from such pain, and this means I was entrusted with a lot and was given important work for my short time on earth. I believe that this is because a part of my purpose is to share what I have learned and am learning (the learning and healing journey is continuous) in hopes that others may heal. These words are me following and believing in purpose.

For example, the woman who produced my poetry video told me a year after that project was completed that I had inspired her to become real with herself. She had been struggling with alcohol but pushed herself into change and has now been sober for over a year.

Healing has no choice but to ripple out when we are real with ourselves and others.

I will share another story that is jam-packed with decolonial love and full-circle healing. It is about embracing and practising our cultural and spiritual ways.

Remember how I was raised strictly Christian? Well, in order for me to heal, I had to incorporate ceremony. It was important for me to remember who I am as a Dane Zaa and Cree woman. As a result, my parents had no choice but to allow this. It meant that they, too, were around ceremony and traditional practices. My parents learned about our culture vicariously through me.

It didn't come without some reservation—pun intended.

I remember that the first time my mom had to sit in a healing circle with me, she didn't want to be in the same room where sage was burning. Her body was tense and her demeanour rigid, but she came to the circle. This was big.

She had gone to a conference the week before where the prominent author and speaker Dr. Martin Brokenleg had presented.

"I listened to Dr. Brokenleg," Mom confided. "He said something about how our children may need different things to heal and make changes. He said some people need culture to heal. So, if this is what my daughter needs, then I will be here for her."

Over the months that followed my last stay at treatment, I smudged daily. At first, I would light the sage or diamond willow fungus outside of her house. It didn't take long before she felt comfortable enough to allow me to smudge indoors. Then, she allowed me to smudge the whole house.

Today, my mother embraces our cultural practices. She has been taking medicine classes. She goes on the land and makes a tobacco offering before picking various roots and leaves. She makes me tea from those medicines. Mom and Dad often make spur-of-the-moment trips into the bush. They return with diamond willow fungus for the family to smudge with. Now, when I walk into her house, my nose is met with the sweet smell of smudge smoke. It smells like decolonized love.

My mom and dad made those choices to reclaim. My healing, however hard, was a small but instrumental part in reintroducing these practices to our family. I am grateful because it changed the course of the generations to come.

My son learns the Dane Zaa language with me as I learn. On long car trips he will point out animals and land features. He is proud to speak the words.

"Grandma!! Gaa [*rabbit*]! Right there!" he yells from the back seat.

My son teaches his grandma the language. Maybe the ancestors have a hand too.

The generations heal themselves.

There is so much power in the act of self-healing.

There is so much power in you, choosing to heal.

You deserve to live a good life. You are worthy of all that is good.

You are worth a thousand horses.

Now go and reclaim that medicine.

To Indigenous Folk Contemplating Suicide

Breathe.
Suck back air.
Keep that oxygen coming,
those pints of blood pumping,
Even if you want to open the rivers
and let them run red right out of you

When you're this close to death
you have everything to lose
and no matter what you think,
you have nothing to prove.

Focus only on the present.
Kick yourself out of yesterdays

and tomorrow,
Well it's not here yet.

Breathe.
Suck back air.
Know that it is the sweetest thing
to ever roll across your tongue.
Savour it, if nothing else seems salvageable
only keep the moment
when days become unmanageable
You come from Indigenous seed
and Ancient forests have laid roots deep
beneath your feet.
You are walking on the bodies of those
who came before you.
Don't ever feel unsupported or alone,
that couldn't be further from the truth.

You come from warriors.
Unflinching and unafraid,
that's how hell and high waters were faced
Blood memories of braves
still run rampant in your veins.

Honour them.

If you are weak,
stuck in a full throttle spin
shook to the core
and you see everyone's life
better off if you're not in it anymore.

Try something different.
Let traditions and ceremony be your medicine.
Let the ancient tongues of your
    grandmothers be your lullaby.
Let prayers be the wings that give you flight.
Let not another light be stolen,
let not another of our own be sacrificed
not another loss to suicide.
Not now.

Breathe.
Suck back air.
Even if you have to do it slowly
with the lights turned off
because it's too hard to live in the light.
Choose life.
I know this sounds cliché
but it's real talk when I say,
things won't always be this way.

Don't let your knees buckle.
It might seem like a stretch right now
but one day you'll be standing proud.
Know that your skin is the most
      beautiful shade of brown
and you are still a warrior
but battles are now fought on different ground

You are most likely feeling the strain and it's hard
whether it be from pulling double shifts,
living daily with the stressors of addicts,
being addicted,
or suffering from some other infliction,

You are more than this.

Breathe.
Suck back air.
Even if it's the hardest thing you have ever had to do.
Don't tell me that you can't,
Because I,
I've been there too.

Afterword

I FIRST CAME "INTO RELATION" WITH HELEN KNOTT when I was co-editing an anthology called *Keetsahnak: Our Missing and Murdered Indigenous Sisters.*[1] Helen wrote us to propose a chapter that would connect the staggering violence against Indigenous women with violence against the land. This work she proposed was theoretically significant and grounded in her home territory near Fort St. John, British Columbia, where Indigenous women suffer and resist the violence of oil fields and male transient

---

1   Kim Anderson, Maria Campbell, and Christi Belcourt, eds., *Keetsahnak: Our Missing and Murdered Indigenous Sisters* (Edmonton: University of Alberta Press, 2018).

workers. As editors, we immediately saw it as essential to the *Keetsahnak* collection because if we are to end violence against Indigenous women we need to see how it is connected to ongoing colonial violence, or, as Helen says in chapter 6 of this book, "how Canada has been failing and continues to fail Indigenous people." Helen was one of the youngest authors to submit an abstract for the *Keetsahnak* book, and we were struck by how much she had already accomplished as an activist and truth teller. We were grateful for her offering.[2]

Then came the memoir, this book.

Helen, reading this book I see you, first, as a gifted writer, a storyteller, and a powerful relation.

I was flattered when you contacted me to share an early draft, asking me for feedback. I remember reading it all in one sitting, turning those pages over on my desk in my office at Laurier University. I was captivated by the power of the writing and the immediacy of voice.

---

2   Helen Knott, "Violence and Extraction: Stories from the Oil Fields," in ibid., 147–60.

This memoir offers a timely and compelling story in an era of increasing attention to the missing and murdered Indigenous women in Canada and elsewhere. Helen's personal story provides us the necessary layers of context and perspective around the lives of Indigenous women lost or nearly lost, for, as she says, "I could have died." We need to know why this happens. As an emerging scholar, Helen gives us the historical background, and as a storyteller she connects it to contemporary and personal manifestations of violence on Indigenous women and lands. These are critical lessons about what fuels the crisis and trauma she describes in the book's opening scene. The vividness of Helen's writing also brings us close to those who are dear, like her friend "Her" and the many other family and community members who were to be our next generation of writers, singers, dancers, mothers. It is a loving testimony to loss, resilience, and resistance, and to the Indigenous families that sustain these realities every day.

Helen, I admire your skill and bravery.

You invoke the core of growing up in a racist, sexually violent world, and then you resist. You write back against the dehumanizing narratives that are typically offered—the statistics or archetypes of women who "deserved it" because of their "lifestyle."

In sharing the heart of your experience, you are crafting our freedom.

This memoir is also a story of addiction and recovery, bringing us inside the experiences that too many know: the self-medicating benders, the shame and self-blame, the terror of relapse, and, if you are one of the lucky ones, the recovery. In Helen's account, we also see how the pain of addiction is compounded when mothering is involved. What I read here, however, is more than a story of loss and recovery. It is a story about the evolution and strength of Indigenous families. Helen's parents, grandmother, and son are vitally present, and so are the generations reaching forward and back. I see the gentle lands of Asu, grandmother, followed by the displacement of generations of parents, not only from homelands but from the beliefs and practices that were rooted in those territories. And then I see a beautiful rendering of how recovery for our peoples is inevitably about reconnecting with Indigenous identities, lands, and cultural and healing practices. For many of us, this is the only way.

Thank you for making this sacrifice of sharing.
Helen, I appreciate how, in your deeply personal artistic production, being "frank and open and honest"

can "encourage the healing journey for others." My heart hears you wanting to hold the pain for others. I appreciate your generosity. And I am certain that your work will ripple out in a healing way—for, as you say, in "being real" with yourself and others, change will happen.

Finally, I am honoured to be included in the launching of this, your first book, and I can't wait to see what you will produce next.

Congratulations!

You make us all proud.

Hiy Hiy. In gratitude.

—KIM ANDERSON, GUELPH, ONTARIO, AUGUST 2018

Acknowledgements

MAMA, YOU ARE THE ABALONE SHELL THAT HOLDS the burning sage. You are the keeper of medicine. You are medicine. I am grateful for your fierce and unyielding love. We have been able to rebuild what was broken, stronger than ever before. Thank you for the countless sacrifices you have made so that I could achieve success. Thank you for being brave and for making me brave enough to truth tell so that others may gain something from it.

Dad. Meathead. Thank you for buying me countless coffees and for listening to me recite poetry and writing. You're my big ol' bear. I am grateful for the cycles you broke in order to give me what you have never had. Your mom, Helen, would be so proud of you.

I am thankful for my asu who has always, always, seen the light in me. Thank you for your endless prayers and your unconditional love. Your praying hands carried me through some hard times.

To the aunties, thank you for being models of strong women for me. When I wanted to give up on everything so long ago, one of you told me, *You won't give up. You want to know why? Because you have no other choice.* Thank you for making success and hard work the only option for me.

To my chosen sisters (friends), Kristy, Juanita, and Addy. Thank you for allowing me to monopolize your phone lines with my madness and for reminding me of my worth when I had forgotten it.

I would like to thank Richard Wagamese, who guided me through the beginning stages of this book. You opened my eyes to seeing myself as a legitimate writer and author. I showed up with a desire to write a book and thirty pages to my name and you helped me transform my vision. Even though you will never be able to see this, I will forever be grateful to you.

Witi Ihimaera, I really did drag myself through the mud on this one but I came out clean. Thank you for helping me build a structure and breathe some life into my book.

To my son, Mathias, whom I hope never reads this book, but if you did and have made it to this part. You are my everything. Atikae nochjay to haklay eenzah and sah. Thank you for choosing me to be your mom. I hope I have been worthy of that blessing.

A huge thanks to Britany Logan and Alison Toews, who sent me money for a laptop when I was a broke single mom and student. The laptop you helped me buy allowed me to go to a writers' program to start this book. Without your faith in me and your kindness, this book may never have been written.

Shelley Wiart, I am forever grateful to you for being an unofficial rep for my manuscript and opening doors for me. You do amazing work raising Indigenous women up.

Thank you to the folks at the University of Regina Press who believed in me and in these words. It has been a long process and I have been grateful for your ability to stay enthused, which kept me enthused after several edits.

Thank you to Hakatah, Creator, God, Jesus, for giving me these words and for the healing so that I was able to write them. I will continue to show up for as long as you continue to use me to relay words in this world. Hiy Hiy. Wuujo Asonalah.

HELEN KNOTT is a Dane Zaa, Nehiyaw, and mixed Euro-descent woman living in Northeastern British Columbia. In 2016 she was one of sixteen global change makers featured by the Nobel Women's Initiative for her commitment to ending gender-based violence. She was named an RBC Taylor Prize Emerging Writer in 2019. This is her first book.

A NOTE ON THE TYPE

This body of this book is set in ADOBE GARAMOND PRO. An Adobe Originals design, and Adobe's first historical revival, Adobe Garamond is a digital interpretation of the roman types of Claude Garamond (1480–1561) and the italic types of Garamond's assistant, Robert Granjon.

Designed by Robert Slimbach in 1989, Adobe Garamond has become a typographic staple throughout the world of desktop typography and design. Slimbach has captured the beauty and balance of the original Garamond typefaces while creating a typeface family that offers all the advantages of a contemporary digital type family.

The accents are set in CHERIE BOMB, a handmade brush font with a punk-rock feeling, but with personality and heart. Cherie Bomb was created by the design studio Great Scott in Stockholm, Sweden.

Text and cover design by Duncan Noel Campbell, University of Regina Press.